Praise for the "Ultimate Guide to HR, Checklists Edition"

"*Ultimate Guide to HR, Checklists Edition* has been incredibly useful for our small non-profit organization—we are so grateful to have this book as a resource for our HR department!"

– Jennifer Ancevski, Non-Profit Deputy Director

"This Book is a 'MUST HAVE' for all small organization management individuals with HR responsibilities and no in-house HR Department. It contains everything you need to know without having to call an expensive law office for counsel, in one, easy-to-use manual of checklists, forms, and educational information."

– PJ Ketcham Robinson, Small Business Owner

"*Ultimate Guide to HR, Checklists Edition* is a great example of a resource that has multiple uses. The tool is perfect for various situations and can be used as is or can be customized to fit just about any unique situation. I recommend this for any person that has anything to do with HR."

– Michael Clark CFP®

"I wish I would have had *Ultimate Guide to HR, Checklists Edition* to help me navigate challenging and routine HR requirements throughout my career. Nothing is more regretful than missing a HR detail that comes back to haunt you. I applaud this easy-to-use reference manual John and Chuck have compiled and recommend it highly. This is an essential resource, a gift that will be a substantial contribution to the improvement of our service industry and valuable helpful assistance to you."

– John Berndt (Former President of Cipriani Hotels and Ritz-Carlton-GM)

"In smaller businesses where one person may wear multiple hats, these checklists come in handy to make sure you are covering all the steps. It is hard when you are doing HR as a function of your job but do not have time to do all the research and these checklists give you the necessary information in a quick format."

– Diane Truett Director of Business Administration

The Ultimate Guide to HR, Checklists Edition

Your Step-by-Step Reference
for Avoiding Costly Mistakes

The Ultimate Guide to HR, Checklists Edition

John Thalheimer, MS Org. Leadership & Chuck Simikian, SHRM-SCP, SPHR

THE ULTIMATE GUIDE TO HR, CHECKLISTS EDITION:
YOUR STEP-BY-STEP REFERENCE FOR AVOIDING COSTLY MISTAKES

John Thalheimer, MS Org. Leadership & Chuck Simikian, SHRM-SCP, SPHR

Copyright © 2024 True Star HR Group

All Rights Reserved

No part of this publication may be reproduced or transmitted in any form or by any means including electronic, mechanical, photocopying, or utilized by any information storage or retrieval system without written permission from the publisher True Star HR. For information about requesting permission to use this material, please contact email@teamathrstories.com.

First Print Edition

ISBN 979-8-9918184-1-4 (Hard Cover)
ISBN 979-8-9918184-0-7 (Paperback)
ISBN 979-8-9918184-2-1 (eBook)

Editing, Interior, and Cover Design by Karen Cronin
www.CroninCreative.com

The Ultimate Guide to HR is dedicated to HR professionals, small business owners, and everyone who manages the employee experience within their organization. Your work is essential to the success of the business. Thank you for all you do to support your organization and its staff. We see you.

The Ultimate Guide to HR: Checklists Edition is approved for 3 SHRM Recertification Credits (PDC's)

To receive your Activity ID, email **credit@TrueStarHR.com**.

Include your name, email address, date of purchase, and location of purchase.

Contents

Foreword: The Power of Checklists 1

Before You Begin 3

Legal Note 4

About the Authors 5

How to be Successful in HR 7
    Human Resources Responsibilities Table... 8
    The Human Resources and Payroll Calendar Checklist 10
    Strategic Planning Worksheet Checklist... 16
    Vision Statement Checklist 20
    Getting HR Right: New HR Directors Checklist 23
    HR Success for Being Perceived as a Positive Resource Checklist 26
    Basic Employment Laws by Number of Employees 28

Human Resources Foundational Documents 33
    Best Practices for Employee Handbooks Checklist 34
    Employee Handbook Contents Checklists 37
    HR Files Checklist 41
    Documentation Reminder Checklist.. 44
    Policy Checklist 47
    Policy Form 49
    Policy Communication Checklist 51
    Business Ethics Checklist... 54
    Job Description Checklist 58
    Building Better Job Description Checklist 65
    Talent Acquisition Checklist 72
    Conducting Remote Interviews Checklist.. 76
    Hiring Process Checklist 79
    Interview and Pre-employment Checklist 85
    New Employee Paperwork... 91
    Offer Letter Checklist 94
    Onboarding Checklist 97
    Simple Interview Scorecard 102

Hiring Independent Contractors 107
    Independent Contractors Checklist 108
    IRS 20 Factor Checklist 112
    ABC Three-Factor Test Checklist 116
    DOL Economic Reality Test 120

Rewarding Employees (Pay & Benefits) 123
- Calculating Employee Pay Checklist 124
- Exempt Status Checklist 127
- Benefits Administration Responsibilities Checklist 132
- Benefits Disclosures and Notifications Checklist 135
- Benefits Open Enrollment Checklist 139
- Leave Policy Checklist 142
- Request for Time Off Form 146
- Training Pay Checklist 149
- Travel Pay Checklist 152

Creating the Best Work Environment 155
- ADA Interactive Process Checklist 156
- ADA Interactive Questions Checklists 160
- Accommodation Request Form 164
- Anti-Harassment & Anti-Discrimination Policy Checklist 165
- Family Medical Leave Act Checklist 169
- Race and Color Discrimination Prevention Checklist 173
- Investigating a Harassment Complaint 176
- Harassment Reporting Form 182
- Workplace Investigations Checklist 186
- The Pregnant Workers Fairness Act Checklist 190
- PUMP Act—Providing Urgent Maternal Protections for Nursing Mothers Act Checklist 193
- Developing an AI Technology Tools Policy Checklist 196
- SAMPLE Policy—The Use of Third-Party AI Tools in the Workplace 201
- Company Holiday Party Legal Considerations Checklist 205
- Difficult Conversation Checklists 210

Managing Remote Workers 215
- Remote Teams Policy Checklist 216
- Remote/Teleworker Agreement Checklist 219
- Home Office Employee Readiness Checklist 222
- Remote Employee Satisfaction Questions Checklist 225

Improving Employee Performance 229
Performance Management Checklist 230
Performance Improvement PIP Form 233
SMART Goals 236
Termination Checklist 239
Exit Interview Questionnaire 244
Using a Performance Improvement Plan (PIP) 248
Stay Interview Checklist 251
Training/Instructional Design Checklist 254
Employee Retention Checklist 257

Keeping the Organization Safe 265
Crisis Response Checklist 266
Employee Safety Program Checklist 270
Merger/Acquisition Due Diligence Checklist 275
Hazards Assessment Identification Checklist 280
OSHA Inspection Prep Checklist 286
OSHA Onsite Visit Inspection Checklist 290
Threat Assessment Checklist 294
Workplace Violence Assessment Checklist 298

Reducing Organizational Risk (Self Audits) 301
EEOC Notification Response Checklist 302
I-9 Error Corrections Checklist 307
I-9 Internal Audit Checklist 311
USERRA Employer Obligations Checklist 315
W-2 Prep Checklist 318

Appendix—Legal Pitfalls 323
Americans with Disabilities (ADA) Legal Pitfalls Checklist 324
FMLA Legal Pitfalls Checklist 326
I-9 Legal Pitfalls Checklist 328

Gratitude 331
The Team at HR Stories 333

State Resources 337

Foreword: The Power of Checklists

The other day I got a phone call from a Director of Human Resources. She was frustrated about a mistake one of her employees had made. They had terminated an employee at the end of the day. Her employee, a manager in the HR Department, had been responsible for terminating the employee and making sure it was done correctly; however, the manager had forgotten to tell the IT Department the employee was dismissed. The employee realized their mistake and sent a blistering email to all the employees, including the CEO. When the Director arrived in the morning, the CEO was the first person she saw. She was not happy.

"How did this happen?" The CEO shouted at the director.

The Director didn't have a good answer. It was standard operating procedures; it should have been done. She called asking me, "How do I make sure her employees get the simple things right?"

"Checklists," I answered.

About two years ago, Chuck and I talked about a book both of us have admired, called *The Checklist Manifesto* by Atul Gawande. The concept was simple when individuals use a checklist; they are less likely to make mistakes. In the book, Dr. Gawande talks about pilots and how they use checklists to ensure they don't make a simple mistake. He wondered if this same procedure would work in his operating rooms. It did, reducing complications and death by over thirty percent.

I love this paragraph where Dr. Gawande explains the importance of the checklist:

> And the question of when to follow one's judgment and when to follow protocol is central to doing the job well—or to doing anything else that is hard. You want people to make sure to get the stupid stuff right. Yet you also want to leave room for craft and judgment and the ability to respond to unexpected difficulties that arose along the way. The value of checklists for simple problems seems self-evident.
> But can they help avert failure when the problems combine everything from the simple to the complex?

The answer he found was yes.

Over a couple of beers, Chuck and I discussed how important it is that we get it right in human resources. Chuck recounted a time when he was the Director of HR at Universal Studio and was in the middle of hiring thousands of employees as Universal Studios expanded its operation. He found that his team of recruiters kept forgetting to check the critical aspects of candidates' applications to see that they had the required information such as contact information, availability, signature, and criminal background checks. Over the years, both of us have made mistakes, had our teams make mistakes, or one of the managers or supervisors make mistakes that have negatively affected our companies.

We kept coming back to the question, "What can we do to ensure small business owners and human resource professionals are getting the simple stuff right?"

"Checklists," we answered in unison.

This book was developed out of our love of the Human Resources profession and giving back to the people we are proud to call colleagues. We know that there are many types of HR Departments... from the person who handles Human Resources duties as part of their job, to the HR department of one, to the large Human Resources departments. Our goal was to create a series of checklists that would be useful to everyone.

We have divided the book into ten different chapters.

1. How to be Successful in HR
2. Human Resources Foundational Documents
3. Talent Acquisition Checklist
4. Hiring Independent Contractors
5. Rewarding Employees (Pay and Benefits)
6. Creating the Best Work Environment
7. Managing Remote Workers
8. Improving Employee Performance
9. Keeping the Organization Safe
10. Reducing Organizational Risk (Self Audits)

Each checklist includes a detailed checklist, legal concerns, and resources. We have also included additional information in the appendix to help you make better employee management decisions.

Our goal is to continue to grow this book by adding more checklists and templates to help us all be more effective at work. Please, if there is a checklist you want us to add, let us know at email@teamathrstories.com.

– John and Chuck

www.teamathrstories.com & www.hrstoriespodcast.com

Before You Begin

Legal Note

Our lawyers wanted you to know that these checklists cannot be considered legal advice. And we wanted you to know that our lawyers are the best. Seriously, no book, class, or facilitator can give you legal advice because they do not know your entire situation. There are thousands of employment laws on the federal, state, and local levels. Although we have over forty years of experience in human resources management between the two of us, we cannot provide professional advice without a complete review of your situation and the circumstances surrounding it. We always recommend that our clients refer to their employment law attorney for problems concerning personnel matters that may arise in the workplace.

Copyright © 2024 True Star HR Group

All Rights Reserved

No part of this publication may be reproduced or transmitted in any form or by any means including electronic, mechanical, photocopying, or utilized by any information storage or retrieval system without written permission from the publisher True Star HR. For information about requesting permission to use this material, please contact email@teamathrstories.com.

HOW TO USE OUR GUIDE

We designed this guide to be easy to use.

Open to the table of contents, find the issue you are trying to solve and go to the appropriate checklist. With over 80 different checklists, this guide helps you navigate HR's toughest challenges from terminating an employee, managing an EEOC complaint, preparing for an interview or merging two HR Departments together.

For those new to handling HR responsibilities, we recommend starting with the HR Responsibility Checklists and Getting HR Right: New Directors Checklist – they provide a overview of HR and the responsibilities of the role. If you are looking to more strategic, start with the Strategic Planning Worksheet, the Vision Planning Checklist, and SMART Goals Checklists, these checklists will help orient your responsibilities to the strategic goals of your organization. If you are looking to deal with more current issues, check out the Developing an AI technology Tools Policy and the Managing Remote Workers section.

Additionally, in every checklist we included resources to help you continue your HR journey and go deeper into the subject matter. In the back we included State Resources to help guide you to the right information for your state.

If you have any questions, please feel free to contact us at email@teamathrstories.com

About the Authors

JOHN THALHEIMER

John Thalheimer is an award-winning management consultant, sought-out workshop facilitator, and author who has helped hundreds of businesses and thousands of professionals transform their potential into extraordinary performance. He is the founder and CEO of True Star Leadership, a business consulting firm focused on workplace performance. John has a master's degree in Organizational Leadership and a Bachelor's in Communication. He is the author of *The Truth About Selling*, a small business guide to marketing.

With over twenty-five years of multi-industry experience, focused on the small business sector, John understands what is necessary to deliver exceptional performance while grounding it in your organization's day-to-day operations. His life-long pursuit is helping emerging leaders managers be better leaders for their organizations. He has worked with LBMC, Center for Non-Profit Management, QVC, Inc., Belmont University, Bloomington Water Reclamation District, Accessibility Service, Inc., Lee Company, Third Coast Comedy, Score Nashville, Turnip Green Creative Reuse, and many more.

Email: john@johnthalheimer.com   Website: https://www.johnthalheimer.com/

CHUCK SIMIKIAN, SPHR, SHRM-SCP

Chuck Simikian is a practicing HR Director and the Founding Partner of Alliance HR Partners, offering human resources consulting and training to businesses nationwide. With over 30 years of corporate HR experience, Chuck has extensive expertise in all aspects of Human Resources, including recruitment, training, employee relations, payroll, and HR compliance. His diverse client base spans industries such as hospitality, themed attractions, retail, resorts, non-profits, and law enforcement.

As a consultant, Chuck emphasizes a "Risk Management" approach to Human Resources, focusing on minimizing legal exposure to entities like the EEOC, DOL, and OSHA. Chuck's background as a front-line manager in operational environments grants him a unique perspective often absent in HR professionals. His clients appreciate his pragmatic, down-to-earth style, which combines hands-on collaboration with flexible energy, enabling him to connect effectively with all organizational levels.

Email: Chuck@alliancehrp.com   Website: https://alliancehrp.com/

How to be Successful in HR

Human Resources Responsibilities Table

PURPOSE:

The following checklist helps new HR practitioners understand an overview of what they will be responsible for managing as human resources professionals for their organization. Not every human resource practitioner will be responsible for everything in this table however, someone in the organization will need to be assigned these tasks.

	HUMAN RESOURCES
Employment Law Compliance	Keeping the Organization and its Executives, Managers, and Employees compliant with employment law through documentation, training, and enforcement
Talent Acquisition	Responsible for assisting with sourcing, screening, and selecting candidates.
Employee Development	Provides Training and Development opportunities and helps identify skill gaps.
Performance Management	Provides guidelines and tools for performance evaluations and assists in the process.
Workplace Policy	Create, update, and enforce workplace policies to ensure compliance.
Organizational Culture	Assist with shaping and promoting the company's culture, values, and mission.
Compensation and Benefits	Designs and administers compensation and benefits programs.
Diversity, Equity, and Inclusion	Develops strategies and initiatives to foster diversity, equity, and inclusion.
Health and Safety	Establishes risk management and safety policies and procedures.
Succession Planning	Identifies high-potential employees and plans for leadership succession.
Employee Engagement	Design engagement programs and surveys.
Data and Analytics	Collects and analyzes HR-related data for strategic decision-making.
Strategic HR Planning	Proactively Partner with senior leadership to understand leadership priorities and create a supportive talent plan to meet those priorities.

LEGAL CONCERNS:

The Human Resources Practitioner and Business work within the confines of employment law at the Federal, State, and Local Law. It is our responsibility to be well-versed in these laws and how they are applicable to our organization. The Team at HR Stories recommends that you seek training and work closely with an employment lawyer to ensure you are getting HR right.

ADDITIONAL RESOURCES:

Below are some federal resources you can use to better understand the laws governing the relationship between employer and employee.

U.S. Department of Labor
www.dol.gov

Job Accomodation Network
www.askjan.org

U.S. Equal Employment Opportunity Commission
www.eeoc.gov

The Americans with Disabilities Act
www.ADA.gov

National Labor Relations Board
www.NLRB.gov

Society for Human Resource Management
www.shrm.org

The Human Resources and Payroll Calendar Checklist

PURPOSE:

One of the most requested checklists the Team at HR Stories receives is a to-do list based on the calendar month. Human Resources and Payroll functions at an organization have strict deadlines and timetables based on employment laws and regulations. In this checklist, we tried to capture as many of those obligations as possible and added in some best practice items as well.

DEFINITIONS:

W-2: W-2 is the official IRS Wage and Tax Statement used to convey to employees their tax statements. It needs to be sent out to the employees before January 31st of the following year.

I-9: The I-9 Form is officially called the Employment Eligibility Verification Form and is used by employers to verify an employee's identity and authorization to work in the United States.

FUTA: Federal Unemployment Tax Act

OSHA: Occupational Safety and Health Administration

PTO: Paid Time Off

The Human Resources and Payroll Calendar Checklist

MONTHLY REMINDERS

- [ ] Each pay period, do a spot check on employees' pay.
- [ ] Run a report on all active employees.
- [ ] Ensure all active employees have the appropriate files.
- [ ] Review terminated files for any expired documentation.
- [ ] Review I-9 files and move terminated employees to the termination binder.
- [ ] Run a report to generate a list of all benefit-eligible employees. Send a reminder email to employees who are eligible in the next month.
- [ ] Do HR Lunch and Learn with managers to discuss hot topics.
- [ ] Spend time with different departments.
- [ ] Meet with the executive team to discuss organizational strategy.

JANUARY

- [ ] Ensure W-2s are properly distributed to employees by January 31st.
- [ ] Ensure 1099s are properly distributed to Independent Contractors by January 31st.
- [ ] File appropriate tax forms (940, 941, 943, 944, & 945).
- [ ] Deposit FUTA taxes by January 31st. (previous quarter).
- [ ] Ensure 1095-B and 1095 C are properly distributed to employees by January 31st.
- [ ] Schedule and hold a refresher course on ethics and professionalism.

FEBRUARY

- [ ] Request a new Form W-4 from employees who claimed exemption from income tax withholding. (Must be received by February 15th.)
- [ ] File Paper Form 8027, Employers Annual Information Return of Tip Income and Allocated Tips by End of the Month. (Digital Form is due March 31st.)
- [ ] Post OSHA Form 300a in a conspicuous location before February 1st until April 30th. Learn more at: www.osha.gov/sites/default/files/OSHA-RK-Forms-Package.pdf
- [ ] Deadline to file ACA Forms 1094-C, 1095C, 1099-MISC without NEC to IRS if paper filling (February 28th).
- [ ] Review PTO Policies and Procedures.
- [ ] Conduct a skills gaps analysis for the workplace.
- [ ] Review and update employee privacy policies and procedures.

The Human Resources and Payroll Calendar Checklist

MARCH

- [ ] Celebrate National Employee Appreciation Day.
- [ ] HIPAA Breach Employee Notification (March 1st).
- [ ] Electronically submit OSHA Form 300A (March 2nd).
- [ ] Deadline to file Form 1099s electronically (March 31st).
- [ ] Employee Safety Training
- [ ] Audit Your I-9s
- [ ] Talk to The Team at HR Stories for Skills and Leadership Training.

APRIL

- [ ] Deposit FUTA taxes by April 30th.
- [ ] Celebrate Administrative Professional Day.
- [ ] Send Summary Plan Description to employees in retirement plans or health benefits covered by the Employee Retirement Income Security Act of 1974 (ERISA).
- [ ] Remove OSHA Form 300a (April 30th).
- [ ] Evaluate employee wellness programs and make adjustments.
- [ ] Do an annual Employee engagement survey (Make suggestions to leadership based on findings).
- [ ] Audit/Storage of separated employee files.
- [ ] Vacation scheduling staff reminders.

MAY

- [ ] Non-Profit Tax Return Deadline, including Form 990.
- [ ] Celebrate International Human Resources Day.
- [ ] Conduct a Benefit Review to ensure competitiveness in the market.
- [ ] Do a benefit survey with employees.
- [ ] Review Summer Weather Protocols.
- [ ] Review and Update Remote work policies, if applicable.
- [ ] Schedule Leadership Offsite for the Fall.

JUNE

- [ ] EE0-1 Data Collection begins.
- [ ] Work with Broker to make changes to Employee benefits.
- [ ] Audit your job descriptions.
- [ ] Conduct a workplace planning session for the following year.
- [ ] Review and update social media policies.
- [ ] Start talent budget planning for the following year.

JULY

- [ ] Deposit FUTA taxes by July 31st.
- [ ] Celebrate Self Care Day.
- [ ] Review your benefit notices or issues as required.
- [ ] Conduct a salary benchmarking analysis.

AUGUST

- [ ] Back-to-School Reminders
- [ ] Remind Employees about Dependent care FSAs and other benefits before school begins.
- [ ] Do roundtables with the employee base.
- [ ] Evaluate the effectiveness of the recruiting process.
- [ ] Submit Talent Budget for the following year.
- [ ] Communicate Open Benefits Enrollment.

SEPTEMBER

- [ ] Celebrate National 401k Day.
- [ ] Celebrate HR Professional Day.
- [ ] Celebrate National Pay Week.
- [ ] Benefit Vendors Presentations
- [ ] Summarize for employees the information that appears in an ERISA plan's Form 5500.
- [ ] Complete a PTO Check—Remind employees to check PTO Balances before Q4.
- [ ] Hold Leadership offsite.
- [ ] Remind employees of Harassment Policies—do additional training.
- [ ] EAP benefit reminder to staff

The Human Resources and Payroll Calendar Checklist

OCTOBER

- [ ] Deposit FUTA taxes by October 31st.
- [ ] Celebrate National Disability Employment Awareness Month.
- [ ] Celebrate National Boss Day.
- [ ] Open Enrollment begins (Date TBD).
- [ ] Review Inclement Weather Protocols.
- [ ] Plan for the end-of-year charitable initiatives or community engagement.
- [ ] Covid, Flu, and RSV immunizations

NOVEMBER

- [ ] Update the Holiday Calendar for the following year.
- [ ] Remind Employees to submit FSA receipts before EOY.
- [ ] Open Enrollment ends (Date TBD).
- [ ] Audit Your Employee Handbook & Policies (change based on new laws and regulations).

DECEMBER

- [ ] Remind employees to submit a new Form w-4 if their filing status, other income, deductions or credits have changed or will change for the next year.
- [ ] Celebrate Giving Tuesday.
- [ ] Year-end Payroll Processing

The Human Resources and Payroll Calendar Checklist

LEGAL CONCERNS:

Federal, State, and Local Employment Laws and Regulations require organizations to do certain tasks by predefined deadlines. This checklist provides you with insights into the requirements of those laws. Laws such as the Fair Labor Standards Act, IRS tax regulations, and Title VII of the Civil Rights Act of 1964.

Your legal liability may be different based on your geographic location, the number of employees you have, the industry you are in, and whether you are a federal or state contractor. Please make sure you review with your employment lawyer to confirm your employer's responsibility.

RESOURCES:

(Circular E)—Employer's Tax Guide
www.irs.gov/pub/irs-pdf/p15.pdf

OSHA
www.osha.gov/sites/default/files/OSHA-RK-Forms-Package.pdf

The Team at HR Stories
teamathrstories.com

John Thalheimer: john@johnthalheimer.com
https://www.johnthalheimer.com/

Chuck Simikian: chuck@alliancehrp.com
https://alliancehrp.com/

EEOC
www.eeocdata.org

Strategic Planning Worksheet Checklist

PURPOSE:

As a Human Resources Leader, you will be asked to create a strategic plan for either your department or yourself. The goal of a good strategic plan is to help guide your efforts over the next few years. The following Strategic Planning Worksheet will provide you with what you should consider to be strategic goals based on your organizational objectives.

NOTES:

Goal Setting is dependent on your work environment and what your leadership's objectives are. In the following worksheet, there are places for you to enter your organization's objectives and reflect on your priorities. The Team at HR Stories believes that there are four major areas of focus every HR practitioner should focus on.

THINKING STRATEGIC: BIG PICTURE

What is the big picture that the organization is focused on or wants to achieve over the next few years?

PEOPLE: BUILDING CULTURE AND A BETTER WORK ENVIRONMENT

What do you need to do to support your employees so that they have the best work environment and culture that supports them in helping achieve the company's goals?

TASKS: OPERATIONAL DRIVERS

What tasks or responsibilities does the human resources team (or you) need to focus on to support your organization to stay in compliance, to meet organizational objectives, and to help employees?

HUMAN RESOURCES METRICS:

What measurements will you use to measure the success of the Human Resources function at your organization?

Strategic Planning Worksheet Checklist

ORGANIZATIONAL OBJECTIVES AS DEFINED BY THE EXECUTIVE LEADER

1. Organizational Vision:

   What does the future look like for the organization?

2. Organizational Mission:

   What is the plan to reach the organizational vision? And what is HR's role with that mission?

3. Organizational Values:

   What values will the organization use to guide its behavior while reaching its objectives?

PRIORITIES BASED ON ORG. OBJECTIVES

STRATEGY: THINKING STRATEGICALLY

- ☐ Team Financial Performance
- ☐ Customer Satisfaction
- ☐ Innovation and Product (Service) Development
- ☐ Operational Efficiency
- ☐ Market Expansion
- ☐ Developing Technology to help your organization grow
- ☐ Strategic Alliances and Partnerships
- ☐ Business Continuity Plans
- ☐ Data, Metrics and Analytics
- ☐ Customer and Market Research

Strategic Planning Worksheet Checklist

PEOPLE: BUILDING CULTURE & BETTER WORK ENVIRONMENT

- ☐ Recognition Programs
- ☐ Positive Work Environment
- ☐ Eliminating Harassment and Discrimination in the workplace
- ☐ Training and Skill Building
- ☐ Diversity, Equity, Including and Belonging
- ☐ Ethical Leadership
- ☐ Employee well-being, including Mental Health
- ☐ Compensation Planning
- ☐ Employee Engagement
- ☐ Team Building and Collaboration
- ☐ Communication and Feedback
- ☐ Workplace Safety

TASKS: OPERATIONAL DRIVERS

- ☐ Process Optimization
- ☐ Supply Chain Management
- ☐ Quality Control
- ☐ Cost Control & Efficiency
- ☐ Resource Allocation
- ☐ Technology Integration
- ☐ Workplace Safety and Compliance
- ☐ Capacity Planning
- ☐ Continuous Improvement
- ☐ Inventory And Asset Management
- ☐ Adherence to Corporate or Industry Standards
- ☐ Customer Service and Operational Excellence

Strategic Planning Worksheet Checklist

"How will you know that your team has been successful?"

POSSIBLE METRICS FOR YOUR TEAM
- [ ] Key Performance Indicators (KPI)
- [ ] Productivity Metrics
- [ ] Quality Metrics
- [ ] Customer Satisfaction and Feedback
- [ ] Employee Engagement and Satisfaction
- [ ] Retention Rates
- [ ] Time-to-Market
- [ ] Cost Metrics
- [ ] Efficiency and Utilization
- [ ] Budget Adherence
- [ ] Innovation Metrics

"If you can't measure it, you can't improve it."

Vision Statement Checklist

PURPOSE

The vision is the desired state of the future being. It answers the question, "What do you want your company to become?" The company's vision statement provides guidance on what executives, managers, and coworkers should work towards. Without one, your company would be a rudderless boat in the open ocean.

DEFINITIONS

Vision: Vision is answering the question, "What do you want your company to become?"

Mission: Mission is answering the question, "What are you going to do to make your vision a reality?"

Vision Statement Checklist

YOUR VISION STATEMENT SHOULD ANSWER THE FOLLOWING QUESTIONS

- [ ] What values are most important to your company?
- [ ] What problem does your company solve?
- [ ] Who does your company serve?
- [ ] What do you do, produce, or serve?
- [ ] Where do you want your company to be in seven years from now?
- [ ] What will you use to measure your success?
- [ ] What do you want to change about your organization?
- [ ] What will motivate your team to achieve this vision?

THE VISION STATEMENT CHECKLIST

- [ ] Review Vision Statement—does it still reflect the desired future state of your company?
- [ ] Talk to executives, managers, and coworkers—what is their engagement with the vision statement?
- [ ] Pull together a vision statement committee to update your visions statement.
- [ ] Test the new vision statement with a portion of your stakeholders. Does it ring true to them? If not, adjust.
- [ ] Hold a company-wide meeting to communicate the new vision statement.
- [ ] Hold team meetings to explain the team's role.
- [ ] Managers hold one-on-one sessions to discuss the new vision statement with employees.
- [ ] Publicize new vision statement through a marketing campaign.
- [ ] Reinforce vision statement in all internal and external communication.

Vision Statement Checklist

LEGAL CONCERNS

Part of the vision statement might include the values of the company. These defined values should be within the parameters of the law.

RESOURCES

True Star Leadership
www.truestarleadership.com

How to Engage Employees Through Your Company Vision Statement
www.entrepreneur.com/article/290803

How to Create a Shared Vision in Your Organization
www.forbes.com/sites/williamcraig/2019/08/27/how-to-create-a-shared-vision-in-your-organization

Getting HR Right: New HR Directors Checklist

PURPOSE

The "Getting HR Right" checklist is designed to guide experienced HR Directors in rapidly assessing and enhancing the Human Resources function within an organization, particularly in situations where previous leadership may have been lacking. This checklist provides a structured approach to identify and address key areas critical for legal compliance, effective employee management, and overall organizational health.

DEFINITIONS

I-9 Compliance: The process of verifying the identity and employment authorization of individuals hired for employment in the United States, ensuring all documentation is accurate and properly filed.

Wage and Hour Compliance: Adherence to laws and regulations related to employee compensation, including minimum wage standards, overtime pay, and proper classification of employees as exempt or non-exempt.

Pay Equity: The practice of providing equal pay for work of equal value, irrespective of gender, race, or other protected characteristics, to promote fairness and compliance with anti-discrimination laws.

Benefit Plan Compliance: Ensuring employee benefit plans adhere to relevant laws and regulations, such as ERISA (Employee Retirement Income Security Act) and ACA (Affordable Care Act).

OSHA Standards: Regulations from the Occupational Safety and Health Administration that must be followed.

EEO Policies: Practices that align with Equal Employment Opportunity guidelines, promoting a workplace free from discrimination based on race, color, religion, sex, national origin, age, disability, or genetic information.

Performance Management: The systematic process of evaluating employee performance with the goal of improving individual and organizational effectiveness.

HR Analytics: The collection and analysis of HR data to inform strategic decision-making, identifying trends and areas for improvement within the HR function.

Getting HR Right: New HR Directors Checklist

IMMEDIATE ACTIONS FOR COMPLIANCE AND LEGAL PROTECTION

COMPLIANCE AUDIT

- [ ] **I-9 Documentation:** Conduct an I-9 audit to ensure proper documentation and storage for active and terminated employees.
- [ ] **Labor Law Postings:** Verify that all required labor law notices are posted and up-to-date.

EMPLOYEE HANDBOOK REVIEW

- [ ] **Policies and Procedures:** Ensure the employee handbook is current, compliant with laws, and accessible to all employees.
- [ ] **Acknowledgment Receipts:** Check that all employees have signed off on the latest handbook.

RECORD-KEEPING

- [ ] **Employee Files:** Audit employee files to ensure they are complete and confidentially maintained.
- [ ] **Separation of Medical Records:** Verify that medical files are stored separately from regular employee files.

WAGE AND HOUR COMPLIANCE

- [ ] **Minimum Wage Compliance:** Ensure all employees are paid at least the minimum wage.
- [ ] **Exempt vs. Non-Exempt Classification:** Review job classifications to ensure compliance with FLSA standards.

PAY EQUITY ANALYSIS

- [ ] **Gender Pay Equity:** Conduct a review to ensure there are no significant disparities in pay between genders in similar roles.
- [ ] **Job Title Consistency:** Check for inconsistencies in job titles and corresponding exempt/non-exempt status.

BENEFIT PLAN COMPLIANCE

- [ ] **ACA Compliance:** Review benefit plans for compliance with the Affordable Care Act.
- [ ] **COBRA Administration:** Ensure proper management of COBRA continuation coverage.

SAFETY AND RISK MANAGEMENT

- [ ] **Workplace Safety:** Verify compliance with OSHA standards and check for any unaddressed workplace safety issues.
- [ ] **Accident Reporting:** Insure there is a process in place to report employee injuries to Workers Comp Insurance.
- [ ] **Workers Compensation:** Review current cases of employee injuries and determine a status on each one.

EEO AND ANTI-DISCRIMINATION POLICIES

- [ ] **EEO Compliance:** Confirm that Equal Employment Opportunity policies are in place and adhered to.
- [ ] **Harassment and Discrimination Training:** Plan mandatory training for all employees.

PERFORMANCE MANAGEMENT REVIEW

- [ ] **Evaluation Process:** Evaluate the current performance review system for effectiveness and legal compliance.

MANAGER MEETINGS

- [ ] **HR Perception:** Schedule meetings with managers and department leaders to understand their perspective on HR functions, support for their needs, and identify areas for improvement.

ADDITIONAL RESOURCES:

Below are some federal resources you can use to better understand the laws governing the relationship between employer and employee.

U.S. Department of Labor (DOL): For comprehensive information on federal labor standards, wage and hour laws, and workplace safety regulations.
www.dol.gov

Equal Employment Opportunity Commission (EEOC): For guidance on anti-discrimination laws and equal employment opportunity regulations.
www.eeoc.gov

Occupational Safety and Health Administration (OSHA): For workplace safety standards and regulations.
www.osha.gov

U.S. Citizenship and Immigration Services (USCIS): For information on employment eligibility verification (Form I-9) and immigration-related employment practices.
www.uscis.gov

HR Success for Being Perceived as a Positive Resource Checklist

PURPOSE

HR departments sometimes face the challenge of being viewed only as policy enforcers or the bearers of bad news. To reshape this perception and be seen as a positive resource, we suggest integrating the following behaviors to build confidence and be seen as an effective resource to management and other employees:

DEFINITIONS

Assertive Communication: The practice of expressing thoughts and needs clearly and respectfully, while also considering the opinions and feedback of others.

Conflict Resolution: Techniques used to address and resolve disagreements in a manner that is fair and considers all parties' perspectives.

Data-Driven Decision Making: The process of making strategic decisions based on data analysis and metrics to enhance HR operations and initiatives.

Diversity and Inclusion: Efforts and policies aimed at creating a workplace that respects and embraces differences, fostering an environment where all employees feel valued and included.

Employee Engagement and Retention: Strategies focused on keeping employees motivated, committed, and satisfied in their roles, thereby reducing turnover and fostering long-term loyalty.

Ethical Leadership: The commitment to lead with integrity and make decisions that uphold the organization's values and ethical standards.

HR Success for Being Perceived as a Positive Resource Checklist

- [ ] **Be a Role Model:** Embody the values and behaviors you wish to see in the organization. Lead by example—everyone is watching! This includes professionalism, integrity, and ethical conduct—follow your own policies.
- [ ] **Follow-up and Follow-through:** Be reliable. Ensure that any queries or issues raised by employees are addressed in a timely manner and that all commitments are met.
- [ ] **Maintain Confidentiality:** Protect sensitive information with the utmost discretion to maintain trust and comply with legal obligations.
- [ ] **Assertive Communication:** Communicate your ideas clearly and confidently without being aggressive.
- [ ] **Relationship Building:** Foster positive relationships with all levels of the organization to build trust and cooperation.
- [ ] **Knowledge of the Law and Procedures:** Be well-versed in employment laws, regulations, and internal procedures to ensure legal compliance and fairness.
- [ ] **Conflict Resolution Skills:** Develop and utilize effective techniques to resolve conflicts in a way that is fair and respectful to all parties involved.
- [ ] **Form and Maintain Good Habits:** Establish productive routines and habits that promote organization, efficiency, and wellness in your work.
- [ ] **Use Checklists:** Implement checklists to ensure that all HR tasks are completed and to maintain order in processes.
- [ ] **Find Reliable Resource/Stay Up To Date:** Be the go-to person for HR-related information, and stay informed about the latest HR trends, technologies, and best practices.
- [ ] **Network with External HR Partners:** Engage with external HR networks for broader insights and support.
- [ ] **Align HR strategies:** Don't practice HR in a "vacuum". Know what the company leader wants. Integrate with the organization's vision and mission, ensuring HR contributes to business objectives.
- [ ] **Adaptability and Flexibility:** Be prepared to adapt strategies and practices to meet the evolving needs of the organization and its workforce.
- [ ] **Policy Development and Implementation:** Ensure that HR policies are up to date, relevant, and effectively implemented.

Basic Employment Laws by Number of Employees

PURPOSE

The Basic Employment Law *Ultimate HR Checklist* provides insight into what laws an employer should be following depending on the number of employees working for them. This *Ultimate HR Checklist* is based on Common Law employees and federal law. Some states and localities may have other thresholds and regulations to adhere to. There may be other laws you need to follow based on the number of independent contractors and different types of workers you have at your company.

NOTE

This document refers to over twenty foundational laws that impact employer and employee relationships. Thousands of other federal, state, and local laws will affect that relationship. You will need to research to be compliant.

Basic Employment Laws by Number of Employees Checklist

AT ONE EMPLOYEE

- [ ] Fair Labor Standards Act (FLSA)—Overtime, Exempt/No-Exempt status, Personnel Records
- [ ] I-9 compliance
- [ ] Equal Pay Act (Lilly Ledbetter Fair Pay Act)
- [ ] HIPAA—Healthcare and Privacy policy. Time limits for keeping specific files and records
- [ ] Occupational Safety and Health Act (OSHA)—Written Hazard Assessment, Fire Prevention Program, Emergency Action Program, Hazardous Chemicals, PPE, Bloodborne Pathogen (if applicable)
- [ ] Employee Polygraph Act
- [ ] National Labor Relations Act
- [ ] USERRA (Uniformed Services Employment and Reemployment Rights Act)
- [ ] The Fair Credit Reporting Act
- [ ] ERISA (Employee Retirement Income Security Act)
- [ ] PUMP Act for nursing mothers

AT 11 EMPLOYEES

- [ ] Fire Prevention and Emergency Action plans to need to be in writing
- [ ] OSHA 300 Logs (if applicable for your industry)

AT 15 EMPLOYEES

- [ ] The Americans with Disabilities Act (ADA)—Prohibiting discrimination against qualified workers with disabilities and mandating reasonable accommodations
- [ ] Title VII of the Civil Rights Act of 1964 (Title VII)—Race, Color, Religion, National Origin, Sex (includes sexual orientation and gender identity)
- [ ] Pregnant Workers Fairness Act- Reasonable accommodations related to pregnancy

AT 20 EMPLOYEES

- [ ] The Age Discrimination in Employment Act of 1967 (ADEA)—40 and over are protected
- [ ] COBRA notifications (Consolidated Omnibus Budget Reconciliation Act)

Basic Employment Laws by Number of Employees Checklist

AT 50 EMPLOYEES

- [ ] The Family and Medical Leave Act (FLMA)—Poster must be placed prominently. Have a clear written policy
- [ ] Affordable Care Act (ACA)

AT 100 EMPLOYEES

- [ ] WARN Act—Requires 60 days advance notice of closing in certain situations. It covers any employer with more than 100 employees
- [ ] EEO-1 Survey Filing—Diversity records. File annually

Basic Employment Laws by Number of Employees Checklist

LEGAL CONCERNS

Organizations are required to follow the employment laws on a federal, state and local level. The laws listed here are the ones that mainly impact small businesses. Please note that there are thousands of employment laws which will vary based on industry, geographical location and other factors.

RESOURCES

Below are some federal resources you can use to understand better the laws that govern the relationship between employer and employee.

U.S. Department of Labor
www.dol.gov

Job Accomodation Network
www.askjan.org

U.S. Equal Employment Opportunity Commission
www.eeoc.gov

The Americans with Disabilities Act
www.ADA.gov

National Labor Relations Board
www.NLRB.gov

Society for Human Resource Management
www.shrm.org (membership site)

Human Resources Foundational Documents

Best Practices for Employee Handbooks Checklist

PURPOSE

Is your employee handbook ready? According to SHRM, employee handbooks are a cornerstone of communication for HR departments and the first line of defense against potential litigation. So, whether starting from "scratch" or auditing your current handbook, use this *Ultimate HR Checklist* to double-check your compliance on the critical issues noted in the following statements.

DEFINITIONS

Employee Handbook: The Employee Handbook guides how an employee should behave in the workplace, defines employee rights and responsibilities, and employer's legal obligations. It will include policies, procedures, mission statements, and other necessary items to ensure your organization complies.

Employment-at-Will: Employment-at-Will is a legal statute that says, "An employer or an employee can sever the relationship for any reason or no reason at all." Please note that there are exceptions to employment-at-will, based on your state laws.

SHRM: Society of Human Resources Manager. According to their website, "SHRM is an organization that creates better workplaces where employers and employees thrive together. As the voice of all things work, workers, and the workplace, SHRM is the foremost expert, convener, and thought leader on issues impacting today's evolving workplaces. With 300,000+ HR and business executive members in 165 countries, SHRM impacts the lives of more than 115 million workers and families globally."

Best Practices for Employee Handbooks Checklist

- [ ] The Handbook was created or reviewed by an HR professional or attorney and customized for our company.
- [ ] The Handbook takes all state or local laws into consideration.
- [ ] All HR and employment policies are in the Handbook.
- [ ] Guidelines are followed consistently in the Handbook when making employment decisions/the practices match the policies.
- [ ] We have an Employment-at-Will statement in our Handbook.
- [ ] We have an Employment-at-Will statement in any job offer letters.
- [ ] Our Progressive Discipline process is flexible to allow for skipping levels as needed based on the severity of the situation.
- [ ] Employee Handbook has a disclaimer that it is not a contract.
- [ ] The Handbook is distributed to all employees.
- [ ] Employees sign an agreement that they have received the latest version of the Employee Handbook.
- [ ] Employees are notified in writing of any changes to the current Handbook.
- [ ] A yearly audit is conducted on the contents of our Employee Handbook.
- [ ] Every two years, an attorney reviews the Employee Handbook.
- [ ] Because it is in writing, our employees understand what incidents and behaviors can result in discipline and termination.
- [ ] The terms "Orientation Period" or "Introductory Period" are used instead of "Probationary Period."
- [ ] We have reviewed the Handbook Contents *Ultimate HR Checklist* to ensure our Handbook contains the necessary policies.
- [ ] Our supervisors and managers have been trained and have an excellent working knowledge of how to use the Handbook in their leadership role.

Best Practices for Employee Handbooks

LEGAL CONCERNS

TITLE VII OF THE CIVIL RIGHTS ACT OF 1964

Title VII prohibits employment discrimination based on race, color, religion, sex, and national origin. All employers in the United States with fifteen or more employees for each working day in each of twenty or more calendar weeks in the current or preceding calendar year.

DISCRIMINATION LAWS INCLUDE BUT ARE NOT LIMITED TO:

- Americans with Disabilities Act
- Age Discrimination in Employment Act
- Pregnancy Act of 1978
- Equal Pay Act of 1963
- Genetic Information Non-discrimination Act
- Don't forget to familiarize yourself with state and local employment laws.

EMPLOYMENT-AT-WILL

An employer or an employee can sever the relationship for any or no reason as long as it is legal. There are exceptions to employment-at-will, including a public policy, implied contract, and covenant-of-good-faith exceptions.

RESOURCES

General Non-Discrimination Policy Tips
www.eeoc.gov/employers/small-business/general-non-discrimination-policy-tips

Employment-at-Will Doctrine
www.law.cornell.edu/wex/employment-at-will_doctrine

At-Will Employment Overview
www.ncsl.org/research/labor-and-employment/at-will-employment-overview.aspx

*All states except Montana

Employee Handbook Contents Checklists

INTRODUCTION

- [ ] Handbook Overview and Purpose
- [ ] Welcome Message from President/CEO
- [ ] At-Will Statement
- [ ] Equal Opportunity Employer
- [ ] Vision/Mission/Values
- [ ] Open Door policy
- [ ] Get Acquainted Period or Introductory Period
- [ ] Union Free Message (if applicable)
- [ ] ADA Accommodation Policy
- [ ] Non-Discrimination and Anti-Harassment Policy
- [ ] Career Opportunities

EMPLOYMENT AND RECORDS

- [ ] Employment Authorization Policy (regarding Form I-9)
- [ ] Employment of Minors
- [ ] Employment of Relatives
- [ ] Confidential Employee Information
- [ ] Definition of Employment Status
- [ ] Outside Employment
- [ ] Personnel Files

WAGE & SALARY ADMINISTRATION

- [ ] Paycheck Errors
- [ ] Paydays, Paychecks and Payroll Deductions
- [ ] Time Clock Procedures

Employee Handbook Contents Checklists

EMPLOYEE BENEFITS PROGRAM

- [ ] Group Health Insurance
- [ ] Performance Evaluations
- [ ] Personal Time Off Policy
- [ ] Vacation Policy
- [ ] Workers' Comp Insurance

WORK CONDITIONS & HOURS

- [ ] Absenteeism and Tardiness
- [ ] Bulletin Boards
- [ ] Meal Breaks
- [ ] Overtime
- [ ] Personal Use of Office Equipment
- [ ] Telephone Use
- [ ] Visitors
- [ ] Work Schedules

LEAVES OF ABSENCE

- [ ] Bereavement Leave
- [ ] Disability Leave
- [ ] Domestic or Sexual Violence Leave (if applicable)
- [ ] Family and Medical Leave of Absence (if applicable)
- [ ] Jury Duty Leave
- [ ] Military Leave of Absence

Employee Handbook Contents Checklists

EMPLOYEE CONDUCT AND DISCIPLINARY ACTION

- [ ] Business Ethics and Conduct
- [ ] Confidential Information
- [ ] Communicating with the Media
- [ ] Conflict of Interest
- [ ] Discipline
- [ ] Dress Codes/Uniforms
- [ ] Drug-Free Workplace Policy
- [ ] E-mail and Communications Policy
- [ ] Employee Dating
- [ ] Employee Internet and Workstation Usage Policy
- [ ] Guarantee of Fair Treatment
- [ ] Prohibition of Kickbacks
- [ ] Safety and Health Policy
- [ ] Smoking
- [ ] Social Media Policy
- [ ] Solicitation and Distribution of Literature
- [ ] Work-Related Injuries
- [ ] Workplace Searches
- [ ] Workplace Violence Policy

Employee Handbook Contents Checklists

LEGAL CONCERNS

- There is no legal requirement to have an Employee Handbook; however, without one, you have no documentation of how you expect employees to behave in your organization.
- Once you add a policy to your handbook, the management team and human resources department must ensure it is being followed.
- Many employment laws and regulations require you to have an employee-communicated policy.
- The employee should be directed to read, understand, and comply with the guidelines within the employee handbook. and should acknowledge with their signature that they understand that responsibility.

RESOURCES

HelpDesk Suites of Compliance Tool-kits
helpdesksuites.com (membership site)

HR Files Checklist

PERSONNEL FILES

Paperwork that should normally belong in an employee's standard personnel file:

- [ ] Employment/Orientation Records
- [ ] Application or resume (with non-confidential info)
- [ ] Offer letter
- [ ] Confidentiality/ non-compete agreement
- [ ] Job description
- [ ] Handbook receipt acknowledgment
- [ ] Drug testing policy acknowledgment
- [ ] Drug testing consent form if applicable (not results)
- [ ] Background check consent form
- [ ] Performance Records
- [ ] Performance evaluation forms
- [ ] Self-evaluations
- [ ] Relevant corrective action documents
- [ ] Performance improvement plans
- [ ] Progress monitoring documents Training Records
- [ ] Required training/certification
- [ ] General new-hire OSHA safety training checklist or acknowledgment
- [ ] Sexual harassment training acknowledgment
- [ ] Federal W-4
- [ ] State withholding forms
- [ ] Pay information
- [ ] Timekeeping records
- [ ] Non-medical wage deduction acknowledgments

HR Files Checklist

INVESTIGATION FILES

A best practice is to keep a separate file of investigations. This would usually be kept by the employee relations manager, HR director, or even the CEO or vice president. These files would be for employee investigations and would hold sensitive information that should not be in any of the files and easily accessed or accidentally accessed by the employee. The final result of employee investigations would normally be kept in the employee file. Any of the documents, notes, meetings, and witness statements should be kept confidential, and in these locked files.

- [ ] Investigation notes and reports
- [ ] Witness statements
- [ ] Investigation interview summaries

MEDICAL/CONFIDENTIAL FILES

These files should be kept separate from any other personnel files and locked in a separate file cabinet with a separate and distinct key from any other files. Utmost care should be taken to prevent these files from being accidentally accessed by anyone outside the HR department contact.

- [ ] Benefits information—Applications/Enrollment forms, Beneficiary Information, Benefit Claims, Correspondence copies, any other benefit-related items
- [ ] Drug test results
- [ ] Medical reports of any sort
- [ ] Doctor notes
- [ ] Workers Comp information
- [ ] FMLA (Family Medical Leave) information
- [ ] Any Leave of Absence information that mentions medical reasons
- [ ] ADA (Americans with Disability Act) requests and related info
- [ ] Medication information
- [ ] Garnishments
- [ ] Any other protected information such as year of birth, medical information, religious beliefs, etc.

HR Files Checklist

LEGAL CONCERNS

THE AMERICANS WITH DISABILITY ACT

This Act requires that disability-related medical information obtained through employment-related examinations or inquiries be kept confidential. This includes, for example, medical exams, return to work documentation, and any data an employee voluntarily discloses as part of an employee health program.

TITLE VII OF THE CIVIL RIGHTS ACT OF 1964

This law makes it illegal to discriminate against someone based on race, color, religion, national origin, or sex. The law also makes it unlawful to retaliate against a person because they complained about discrimination, filed a charge of discrimination, or participated in an employment discrimination investigation or lawsuit. The law also requires that employers reasonably accommodate applicants' and employees' sincerely held religious practices unless doing so would impose an undue hardship on the operation of the employer's business.

HIPAA: HEALTH INSURANCE PORTABILITY AND ACCOUNTABILITY ACT

Requires employers to protect medical or health plan records if the employee is a health plan member.

RESOURCES

Recordkeeping Requirements
www.eeoc.gov/employers/recordkeeping-requirements

State Laws on Access to Your Personnel File
www.nolo.com/legal-encyclopedia/free-books/employee-rights-book/chapter5-2.html

Documentation Reminder Checklist

PURPOSE

HR documentation is a fundamental tool for maintaining compliance, fostering effective communication, managing employee relations, and supporting various HR functions within an organization. It helps ensure compliance with local, state, and federal labor laws and regulations. It is essential for maintaining accurate and up-to-date employee records. It is key to the performance management process. It helps resolve workplace conflicts and disputes. This checklist is a reminder of documentation that should be taking place in an organization with respect to the human resources function.

NOTE

This is not a comprehensive list, but it should give the reader an understanding of all the types of information that should be documented.

Documentation Reminder Checklist

- [ ] Supervisors and Managers should document employee interactions, particularly those that are out of the norm.
- [ ] Supervisors and Managers should document all performance conversations, whether to praise, reward, provide feedback, or discipline an employee.
- [ ] Track all training and development workshops, seminars, class participation, and attendees.
- [ ] Capture all time-off requests, including vacation, personal time off, sick time, bereavement, family and medical leave, etc.
- [ ] Keep doctor's notes for time off requests.
- [ ] Document the interactive process, including requests for accommodation, medical information, interviews with employees and managers, etc. (See ADA Interactive checklist.)
- [ ] Document any voluntary payroll withholding requests, including insurance, savings, union dues, and direct deposits.
- [ ] Capture documents for involuntary payroll withholding requests, such as garnishments.
- [ ] Store any interview notes, taking my supervisors, managers, and HR personnel involved in the hiring process.
- [ ] Document Drug Tests.
- [ ] Store I-9s for the appropriate time period.
- [ ] Store W-4s for four years after the information was used on an IRS tax return. (Typically, five years after the termination of an employee).
- [ ] Store all notes from Employee investigations from allegations dealing with Discrimination and Harassment in the workplace.

Documentation Reminder Checklist

LEGAL CONCERNS

THE AMERICANS WITH DISABILITY ACT

This Act requires that disability-related medical information obtained through employment-related examinations or inquiries be confidential. This includes, for example, medical exams, return to work documentation, and any data an employee voluntarily discloses as part of an employee health program.

TITLE VII OF THE CIVIL RIGHTS ACT OF 1964

This law makes it illegal to discriminate against someone based on race, color, religion, national origin, or sex. The law also makes it unlawful to retaliate against a person because they complained about discrimination, filed a charge of discrimination, or participated in an employment discrimination investigation or lawsuit. The law also requires that employers reasonably accommodate applicants' and employees' sincerely held religious practices unless doing so would impose an undue hardship on the operation of the employer's business.

HIPAA: HEALTH INSURANCE PORTABILITY AND ACCOUNTABILITY ACT

Requires employers to protect medical or health plan records if the employee is a health plan member.

RESOURCES

Recordkeeping Requirements
www.eeoc.gov/employers/recordkeeping-requirements

State Laws on Access to Your Personnel File
www.nolo.com/legal-encyclopedia/free-books/employee-rights-book/chapter5-2.html

Policy Checklist

PURPOSE

Policies are the guidance organizations provide to their workforce. They detail the rights and responsibilities of both employee and employer. Procedures will include attendance, leave, dress code, anti-harassment and discrimination, social media usage, and zero-tolerance for workplace violence. They align expectations and are the behavioral manual for your coworkers, managers, and executives.

DEFINITIONS

Employer Policy: Company policies and procedures are basic guidelines on how an employer expects an employee to behave in the workplace. Typically these policies and practices are kept in the employee handbook for the employee to access whenever necessary.

Policy Checklist

- [ ] Ask, "What behaviors do you expect from your employees?"
- [ ] Clearly define the problem that needs to be addressed
- [ ] Prioritize compliance (legal concerns), include a legal representative if necessary
- [ ] Check for existing policies
- [ ] Identify impacted group or team
- [ ] Develop new policy-make sure it meets company standards
- [ ] Use straightforward language
- [ ] Easy to understand
- [ ] All acronyms are defined
- [ ] Not too restrictive
- [ ] Do not include information that can be quickly outdated, e.g., a person's name; instead, use position title
- [ ] See Form below
- [ ] Review with impacted team leaders or executive team members
- [ ] Revise as necessary
- [ ] Review with legal representation
- [ ] Communicate and train impacted team

*Please note there is a difference between policy and procedure.

Policy Form

TITLE:

The policy title should convey what the policy is about.

PURPOSE OF THE POLICY:

What is the reason the company is instituting this policy?

DETAILED POLICY:

Complete policy content. What the policy is. Who it impacts. When it takes effect. Who to go to with concerns.

DEFINITIONS:

Define any acronyms or words that might confuse, such as policy or procedure.

COMPLIANCE:

Include any legal statute or company compliance regulation.

RELATED POLICIES:

Include cross-references to any other policies that might impact the interpretation of the said policy.

IMPLEMENTATION:

Procedures and Reference material to be used to carry out the policy's intent.

Policy Form

LEGAL CONCERNS

All written policies must fall within the legal framework of federal, state, and local laws.

RESOURCES

Sample Employee Handbook

www.501commons.org/resources/tools-and-best-practices/human-resources/sample-employee-handbook-national-council-of-nonprofits

NCSL Research & Policy

www.ncsl.org/research/labor-and-employment/disability-101-employment-policies-and-etiquette.aspx

Employee Policies & Procedures

smallbusiness.chron.com/employee-policies-procedures-2703.html

Policy Communication Checklist

PURPOSE

Circumstances change. You may need to update and communicate new policies to your employees. At *Ultimate HR Checklist*, we recommend that every organization has a dynamic employee handbook to store and share organization guidelines and policies. When a policy changes, it is imperative that you communicate and document the update to all employees that it impacts.

DEFINITIONS

Employer Policy: Company policies and procedures are basic guidelines on how an employer expects an employee to behave in the workplace. Typically these policies and procedures are kept in the employee handbook for the employee to access whenever necessary.

Policy Communication Checklist

- [ ] Update policy
- [ ] Review any concerns with leadership, update if necessary
- [ ] Review with an employment lawyer to make sure it is legal and doesn't cause a disparate impact
- [ ] Communicate to impacted team members (do all steps below)
- [ ] General email—include the purpose of change, new policy, date of the change, actions required, and how to raise concerns
- [ ] Present in-staff meetings
- [ ] A one-on-one conversation with impacted team members
- [ ] Communicate to those directly affected
- [ ] Provide a means for employees to raise concerns
- [ ] Listen to employees and make changes if necessary (review any changes with executives and legal team)
- [ ] Have all employees sign and date the new policy, acknowledging that they are responsible for following the latest guidance
- [ ] Add the policy to the employee handbook—orientate new employees
- [ ] File signature documentation in the appropriate files
- [ ] Provide the necessary skill-building and training for employees
- [ ] Reinforce policy through increased communication via posters, emails, and other visual and written communication
- [ ] Reinforce policy by recognizing employees' efforts

BEST COMMUNICATION PRACTICES

- [ ] Keep it simple and direct
- [ ] Don't rely on just one method of communication
- [ ] Use the right person to communicate—Employees look to their immediate supervisor to share how it will impact them
- [ ] Repeat for comprehension
- [ ] Make sure employees understand the why
- [ ] Make certain employees understand what's in it for them (WIIFM)
- [ ] Listen and change the policy if necessary

Policy Communication Checklist

LEGAL CONCERNS

All written policies must fall within the legal framework of federal, state, and local laws.

RESOURCES

Sample Employee Handbook
www.501commons.org/resources/tools-and-best-practices/human-resources/sample-employee-handbook-national-council-of-nonprofits

NCSL Research & Policy
www.ncsl.org/research/labor-and-employment/disability-101-employment-policies-and-etiquette.aspx

Employee Policies & Procedures
smallbusiness.chron.com/employee-policies-procedures-2703.html

Business Ethics Checklist

PURPOSE

The Business Ethics *Ultimate HR Checklist* provides employer reminders on keeping their organization ethical. Building and maintaining a culture of ethics is an ongoing process, not a quick fix. It is not easy, but it may be the most critical step in sustaining a healthy organization.

DEFINITIONS

Business Ethics: Business Ethics are values and standards used to govern how the business will operate, especially on how employees and customers will be treated within the organization. Business ethics can be seen in the way coworkers relate to each other and how the business makes decisions around corporate governance. In certain instances, business ethics revolve around the legal landscape in which the organization does business.

Business Ethics Checklist

SIX STEPS TO MAKING ETHICAL DECISIONS

1. Recognize an ethical issue (Corporate Governance, insider trading, bribery, discrimination, corporate social responsibility, social justice, and fiduciary responsibility)
2. Get the facts (don't jump to conclusions)
3. Formulate and evaluate alternative actions
4. Seek input or additional assistance
5. Decide and test it
6. Act and reflect on the outcome

ETHICS POLICY AREAS TO CONSIDER

- ☐ Conduct with Vendors—Gifts and Gratuities
- ☐ Conduct with Members, Associates, & Customers
- ☐ Undisclosed commissions, Kickbacks, Bribes, Etc.
- ☐ Political Contributions and Activities
- ☐ Procedures for Addressing the Conflict of Interest
- ☐ Violations of the Business Ethics and Conduct Policy
- ☐ Financial Statements
- ☐ Responsibility
- ☐ Nondisclosure of Confidential and Proprietary Business Information
- ☐ Professional Relationships
- ☐ Alternate Reporting Procedures
- ☐ Other Potential Issues within your Industry

Business Ethics Checklist

HR'S ROLE IN CREATING AN ETHICAL ORGANIZATION

- [ ] Develop policies–have written standards of conduct
- [ ] Communicate with employees
- [ ] Provide training on ethics and company policies
- [ ] Handle questions and complaints
- [ ] Create a feedback or reporting system
- [ ] Support and communicate a retaliation-free atmosphere for reporting violations
- [ ] Assist organization leaders with resolving difficult situations
- [ ] Add ethical behaviors to the performance appraisal
- [ ] Enforce discipline for ethical violations

ETHICAL BEHAVIOR PRACTICES BY MANAGEMENT

- [ ] Set an example for the team–walk the talk
- [ ] Publicly champion the importance of ethics
- [ ] Develop a personal set of values
- [ ] Make decisions based on values
- [ ] Establish zero tolerance for ethical violations
- [ ] Recognize and support honest employees

Business Ethics Checklist

LEGAL CONCERNS

TITLE VII OF THE CIVIL RIGHTS ACT OF 1964

Title VII prohibits employment discrimination based on race, color, religion, sex, and national origin. All employers in the United States with fifteen or more employees for each working day in each of twenty or more calendar weeks in the current or preceding calendar year.

IMMIGRATION REFORM AND CONTROL ACT OF 1986

Under federal law, employers must verify that all employees are legally authorized to work in the United States of America and keep forms verifying that employees are legally authorized to work in the USA.

OCCUPATIONAL SAFETY AND HEALTH

According to the general clause of OSHA, employers are required to have a workplace free from recognized hazards that may cause death or serious harm. It is unethical to disregard or blatantly ignore the safety of our team members.

RESOURCES

U.S. Equal Employment Opportunity Commission
www.eeoc.gov

Occupational Safety and Health Administration
www.osha.gov

U.S. Citizenship and Immigration Services
www.uscis.gov

Journal of Business Ethics
www.springer.com/journal/10551

List of Ethical Issues in Business
smallbusiness.chron.com/list-ethical-issues-business-55223.html

U.S. Small Business Administration
www.sba.gov

Job Description Checklist

PURPOSE

Job descriptions have so many functions within HR. They are the core of the HR process and touch many other related aspects —creating job ads, evaluating employee performance, aligning expectations, and evaluating accommodation requests related to the Americans with Disabilities Act. Putting together a solid job description is not easy, but this *Ultimate HR Checklist* can help guide the way.

DEFINITIONS

Job: A paid position of regular employment.

Employ: By statutory definition, the term "employ" includes "to suffer or permit to work." The workweek ordinarily has all time during which an employee is required to be on the employer's premises, on duty, or at a prescribed workplace.

"Workday," in general, means the period between the time on any particular day when such employee commences their "principal activity" and the time on that day at which they cease such principal activity or activities; therefore, the workday may be longer than the employee's scheduled shift, hours, a tour of duty, or production line time.

Job Description Checklist

ANALYZE THE JOB

- [ ] Ask the employee about their required tasks
- [ ] Discuss with the employee the knowledge, abilities, and skills needed to be successful at the job
- [ ] Observe employees at their workstation
- [ ] Record employee at work as appropriate
- [ ] Ask stakeholders about employee's required tasks
- [ ] Capture the tasks the employee is responsible for doing
- [ ] Take note of all tools, equipment, and process used

BUILD THE JOB DESCRIPTION

- [ ] Name the position
- [ ] Explain the purpose of the job
- [ ] Describe the tasks, responsibilities, and expected outcomes of the job
- [ ] Decide on the level of the employee
- [ ] Note if they will be supervising anyone

DESCRIBE THE QUALIFICATIONS FOR THE JOB

- [ ] Explain the required knowledge needed to be successful in the job
  - General Knowledge (Common Sense)
  - Customer Service Knowledge
  - Technical or Job Specific Knowledge
  - Supervisorial Knowledge
  - Organization Knowledge
  - Legal Knowledge

Job Description Checklist

- ☐ Explain the required abilities needed to be successful in the job
  - General Knowledge (Common Sense)
  - Customer Service Knowledge
  - Technical or Job Specific Knowledge
  - Supervisorial Knowledge
  - Organization Knowledge
  - Legal Knowledge
- ☐ Capture the experience needed to be successful in the job
  - Years doing the exact work
  - Years doing similar work
  - Years working in the industry
- ☐ Capture the necessary training to be successful in the job
  - Certification
  - Education Level
  - Adjacent Training
- ☐ Capture the necessary capabilities to be successful in the job
  - Physical capabilities
    – Sitting or standing
    – Lifting Load
    – Temperature variation
    – Length of work shift
    – Movement
    – Senses Used
  - Mental capabilities
    – Communication
    – Conflict
    – Personal Interaction
    – Focus
    – Commitment
    – Deal with Pressure and Deadlines

DETAIL THE WORK CONTEXT

- [ ] Explain the work context the employee will be working in
  - Hot/cold
  - Inside/outside
  - Noise level
  - Lighting
  - Workstation/Office/Cubicle
- [ ] Describe the job's social atmosphere
  - Close contact with coworkers
  - Works with public
  - Works alone
- [ ] Note all the tools and equipment that will be used
  - Computer Equipment
  - Manual Tools
  - Power Tools
  - Phone Equipment
  - Safety Equipment

SETTING COMPENSATION PACKAGE

- [ ] Fair Labor Standard Act (Non-Exempt or Exempt Employee)
  - Non-Exempt are paid overtime for hours over 40 (State law may vary)
  - Exempt employees are not paid overtime
  - Assume all Employees are Non-Exempt until you have answered the following questions.
  – Is their salary range below the standard salary level in your area?
  – Will they be paid based on the hours worked? If the answer is yes—most likely, they are non-exempt employees.
  – Will the amount they are paid weekly vary? If the answer is yes—most likely, they are non-exempt employees.
  – Do they meet the "duties" requirement for exemption as stated in the FLSA? There are six possible exemptions. Your employee must meet the criteria laid out in the FLSA to be an exempt employee. For more information, go to The Wages and Hour Division at www.dol.gov.

Job Description Checklist

☐ Salary Structure
- Pay based on responsibilities and hours worked
- Compare position to others of similar responsibilities and experience requirements
- Factor in # of employees reporting to the position
- Use www.onetonline.org for salary information

CREATE CONSISTENCY

☐ Use the same format for all job descriptions in the organization
☐ Create a hierarchy within your organization
☐ Audit Job Descriptions once every two years
☐ Do compensation reviews every four years

Job Description Checklist

LEGAL CONCERNS

THE AMERICANS WITH DISABILITY ACT, INCLUDING THE ADAAA

Under Title I of the Americans with Disability Act, a person is said to have a disability if they have a physical or mental impairment that substantially limits one or more of their major life activities. It also states that a Qualified Individual with a Disability is an individual who meets the skills, experience, education, and other job-related requirements of a position held or desired with or without reasonable accommodations and can perform the job's essential functions.

FAIR LABOR STANDARD ACT (FLSA)

Created in 1938, the Fair Labor Standard Acts sets the policies we use today to set proper compensation for our employees, including the federal minimum wage, the standard salary level, child labor laws, what is considered hours worked, correct record keeping, and the difference between those employees who receive overtime and those that do not.

CIVIL RIGHTS ACT OF 1964 (TITLE VII)

Protects individuals in various protected classes from discrimination throughout the employee life cycle. If we intentionally or unintentionally treat individuals differently because they are members of a protected class, this is discrimination. The job description sets the qualifications necessary to be hired for a particular job.

BONA FIDE OCCUPATION QUALIFICATION (BFOQ)

In some circumstances, an employer can discriminate based on sex, age, and religion in its hiring process if there is a bona fide occupational qualification that can only be met by a particular class of people; think hiring a male model to model a line of male clothing.

Job Description Checklist

RESOURCES

U.S. Department of Labor
www.dol.gov

U.S. Equal Employment Opportunity Commission
www.eeoc.gov

O*NET OnLine
www.onetonline.org

Job Accomodation Network
askjan.org

CareerOnestop Toolkit
www.careeronestop.org/toolkit/toolkit.aspx

Society for Human Resource Management
www.shrm.org (membership)

Building Better Job Description Checklist

PURPOSE

One of the foundational documents of organizational success is the job description; however, creating job descriptions that truly reflect what an employee is doing in their role can be overwhelming. The following checklist provides information to help make job descriptions more accurate.

NOTES:

Soft Skills: Many employers value workers with soft interpersonal and thinking skills needed to interact successfully with people and perform efficiently and effectively in the workplace.

Abilities: Abilities are enduring attributes of the individual that influence performance.

Knowledge: Knowledge is organized sets of principles and facts applied in general domains.

Work Context: Work context refers to the physical and social factors that influence the nature of work.

Work Styles: Work styles are personal characteristics that can affect how well someone performs a job.

Work Values: Work values are global aspects of work that are important to a person's satisfaction.

Building Better Job Description Checklist

SOFT SKILLS:

- [ ] **Coordination:** Adjusting actions in relation to others' actions
- [ ] **Instructing:** Teaching how to do something
- [ ] **Negotiation:** Bringing others together and trying to reconcile differences
- [ ] **Persuasion:** Persuading others to change their minds or behaviors
- [ ] **Service Orientation:** Actively looking for ways to help people
- [ ] **Social Perceptiveness:** Being aware of others' reactions and understanding why they react as they do.
- [ ] **Active Learning:** Understanding new information's implications for current and future problem-solving and decision-making.
- [ ] **Active Listening:** Giving full attention to what other people are saying, taking time to understand the points being made, asking questions as appropriate, and not interrupting at inappropriate times.
- [ ] **Complex Problem Solving:** Identifying complex problems and reviewing related information to develop and evaluate options and implement solutions.
- [ ] **Critical Thinking:** Using logic and reasoning to identify strengths and weaknesses of alternative solutions, conclusions, or problem approaches.
- [ ] **Judgment and Decision-Making:** Considering the relative costs and benefits of potential actions to choose the most appropriate one.
- [ ] **Learning Strategies:** Selecting and using training/instructional methods and procedures appropriate for the situations when learning or teaching new things.
- [ ] **Monitoring:** Monitoring/Assessing the performance of yourself, other individuals, or organizations to make improvements or take corrective action.
- [ ] **Time Management:** Managing one's own time and the time of others.

ABILITIES:

- [ ] **Cognitive Abilities:** Abilities that influence the acquisition and application of knowledge in problem-solving, such as attentiveness, idea generation, memory, and spatial and verbal abilities.
- [ ] **Physical abilities:** Abilities that influence strength, endurance, flexibility, balance, and coordination, such as endurance, flexibility, balance, coordination, and physical strength abilities.
- [ ] **Psychomotor Abilities:** Abilities related to the capacity to exert force, such as control movement, fine manipulation, and reaction time and speed abilities.
- [ ] **Sensory Abilities:** Abilities that influence visual, auditory, and speech perception.

Building Better Job Description Checklist

KNOWLEDGE:

- [ ] **Arts and Humanities:** Knowledge of facts and principles related to the branches of learning concerned with human thought, language, and the arts such as language, fine arts, history, and philosophy.
- [ ] **Business Management:** Knowledge of principles and facts related to business administration and accounting, human and material resource management in organizations, sales and marketing, economics, and office information and organizing systems.
- [ ] **Communication:** Knowledge of the science and art of delivering information.
- [ ] **Education and Training:** Knowledge of principles and methods for curriculum and training design, teaching and instruction for individuals and groups, and the measurement of training effects.
- [ ] **Engineering and Technology:** Knowledge of the design, development, and application of technology for specific purposes.
- [ ] **Health Services:** Knowledge of principles and facts regarding diagnosing, curing, and preventing disease and improving and preserving physical and mental health and well-being.
- [ ] **Law and Public Safety:** Knowledge of regulations and methods for maintaining people and property free from danger, injury, or damage; the rules of public conduct established and enforced by legislation; and the political process establishing such rules.
- [ ] **Manufacturing and Production:** Knowledge of principles and facts related to the production, processing, storage, and distribution of manufactured and agricultural goods.
- [ ] **Mathematics and Science:** Knowledge of the history, theories, methods, and applications of the physical, biological, social, mathematical, and geography.
- [ ] **Transportation:** Knowledge of principles and methods for moving people or goods by air, rail, sea, or road, including the relative costs and benefits.

Building Better Job Description Checklist

WORK CONTEXT:

☐ **Interpersonal Relationships:** This category describes the context of the job in terms of human interaction processes.

- *Communication:* Types and frequency of interactions with other people required for this job.
- *Conflictual Contact:* Amount of conflict that the worker will encounter as part of this job.
- *Responsibility for Others:* Amount of responsibility the worker has for other workers as a part of this job.
- *Role Relationships:* Importance of different types of interactions with others both inside and outside the organization.

☐ **Physical Work Conditions:** This category describes the work context as it relates to the interactions between the worker and the physical job environment.

- *Body Positioning:* Amount of time the worker will spend in various physical positions on this job.
- *Environmental Conditions:* Description of extreme environmental conditions the worker will be placed in as part of this job.
- *Job Hazards:* Descriptions of types of hazardous conditions the worker could be exposed to as part of this job. This includes the frequency of exposure and the likelihood and degree of injury if exposed.
- *Work Attire:* Dress requirements for this job.
- *Work Setting:* Description of the worker's physical surroundings as part of this job.

☐ **Structural Job Characteristics:** This category involves the relationships or interactions between the worker and the structural characteristics of the job.

- *Competition:* Amount of competition that the worker will face as part of this job.
- *Criticality of Position:* Amount of impact the worker has on final products and their outcomes.
- *Pace and Scheduling:* Description of the role that time plays in the way the worker performs the tasks required by this job.
- *Routine versus Challenging Work:* The relative amounts of routine versus challenging work the worker will perform as part of this job.

WORK STYLE:

- [ ] **Achievement Orientation:** The job requires personal goal setting, trying to succeed at those goals, and striving to be competent in one's own work.
  - *Achievement/Effort:* The job requires establishing and maintaining personally challenging achievement goals and exerting effort toward mastering tasks.
  - *Initiative:* The job requires a willingness to take on responsibilities and challenges.
  - *Persistence:* The job requires persistence in the face of obstacles.
- [ ] **Adjustment:** The job requires maturity, poise, flexibility, and restraint to cope with pressure, stress, criticism, setbacks, personal and work-related problems, etc.
  - *Adaptability/Flexibility:* Job requires being open to change (positive or negative) and to considerable variety in the workplace.
  - *Self-Control:* The job requires maintaining composure, keeping emotions in check, controlling anger, and avoiding aggressive behavior, even in very difficult situations.
  - *Stress Tolerance:* The job requires accepting criticism and dealing calmly and effectively with high-stress situations.
- [ ] **Conscientiousness:** The job requires dependability, commitment to doing the job correctly and carefully, and being trustworthy, accountable, and attentive to details.
  - *Attention to detail:* The job requires being careful about detail and thorough in completing work tasks.
  - *Dependability:* The job requires being reliable, responsible, and dependable and fulfilling obligations.
  - *Integrity:* The job requires being honest and ethical.
  - *Independence*: The job requires developing one's own ways of doing things, guiding oneself with little or no supervision, and depending on oneself to get things done.
- [ ] **Interpersonal Orientation:** The job requires being pleasant, cooperative, sensitive to others, easy to get along with, and preferring associating with other organization members.
  - *Concern for others:* The job requires being sensitive to others' needs and feelings and understanding and helpful.
  - *Cooperation:* The job requires being pleasant with others on the job and displaying a good-natured, cooperative attitude.
  - *Social Orientation:* The Job requires preferring to work with others rather than alone and being personally connected with others on the job.
- [ ] **Practical Intelligence:** The job requires generating useful ideas and thinking things through logically.
  - *Analytical Thinking:* The job requires analyzing information and using logic to address work-related issues and problems.
  - *Innovation:* The job requires creativity and alternative thinking to develop new ideas for and answers to work-related problems.
- [ ] **Social Influence:** The job requires having an impact on others in the organization and displaying energy and leadership.
  - *Leadership:* The Job requires a willingness to lead, take charge, and offer opinions and direction.

Building Better Job Description Checklist

WORK VALUES:

- ☐ **Achievement:** Occupations that satisfy this work value are results-oriented and allow employees to use their strongest abilities, giving them a feeling of accomplishment. Corresponding needs are Ability Utilization and Achievement.

- ☐ **Independence:** Occupations satisfying this work value allow employees to work independently and make decisions. Corresponding needs are Creativity, Responsibility, and Autonomy.

- ☐ **Recognition:** Occupations that satisfy this work value offer advancement and potential for leadership and are often considered prestigious. Corresponding needs are Advancement, Authority, Recognition, and
Social Status.

- ☐ **Relationships:** Occupations that satisfy this work value allow employees to provide service to others and
work with co-workers in a friendly, non-competitive environment. Corresponding needs are Co-workers, Moral Values, and Social Service.

- ☐ **Support:** Occupations that satisfy this work value offer supportive management that stands behind employees. Corresponding needs are Company Policies, Supervision: Human Relations and **Supervision: Technical.**

- ☐ **Working Conditions:** Occupations that satisfy this work value offer job security and good working conditions. Corresponding needs are Activity, Compensation, Independence, Security, Variety and Working Conditions.

Building Better Job Description Checklist

LEGAL CONCERNS

When building job descriptions, they should reflect as accurately as possible what the employee does and is required to know to excel at that role within your organization. Job descriptions are relied on during the hiring and selection process and performance management to be in compliance with laws such as the Americans with Disabilities Act and the Family Medical Leave Act. They are also used when terminating employees for not performing their job to expectations.

RESOURCES:

O*NET Online
www.onetonline.org

Occupational Outlook Handbook
www.bls.gov/ooh

Talent Acquisition Checklist

PURPOSE

Recruiting, selecting, and hiring employees can be a complicated process with many moving parts. The Purpose of the Talent Acquisition Checklist is to create a simple system to make sure all the appropriate steps are completed to increase the chances of hiring the best employees and to provide documentation.

DEFINITIONS

Hiring Manager: The hiring manager is the manager who is responsible for deciding the necessary qualifications for an opening within the organization and deciding on who to hire with the help of the human resources team.

Phone Screening: Phone screening is the process where candidates are filtered down via questions if they don't meet the basic requirements of the role.

Fair Credit Reporting Act: The purpose of the Fair Credit Reporting Act is to require that consumer reporting agencies adopt reasonable procedures for meeting the needs of commerce for consumer credit, personnel, insurance, and other information in a manner that is fair and equitable to the consumer, regarding the confidentiality, accuracy, relevancy, and proper utilization of such information.

Employment-at-Will: In all states except Montana, there is a statute called Employment-at-Will, which says that the employer or the employee can sever the relationship at any time for any reason, with or without notice (as long as it is legal).

Talent Acquisition Checklist

- [ ] Supervisor or Manager completes new employee request form.
- [ ] HR and senior leadership approve the request.
- [ ] The Request is sent to the HR Recruiter or person responsible for recruiting new staff.
- [ ] The HR Recruiter reviews the request for understanding.
- [ ] The HR Recruiter reviews the job description to build the job postings.
- [ ] The job posting is written.
- [ ] The job posting is approved by the hiring manager and HR lead.
- [ ] The job posting is published on the company website, social media feeds, and job posting boards.
- [ ] Candidates send in their application and resume for the position.
- [ ] Candidates' information is sorted and filtered based on criteria set in the employee request form.
- [ ] Appropriate candidates are sent to the hiring manager for first approval.
- [ ] The hiring manager and HR partner select candidates to be phone screened.
- [ ] Phone screening interviews are scheduled.
- [ ] HR phone screens candidates for education, certification, experience, etc.
- [ ] The candidate pool is thinned by HR based on criteria set in the employee request form.
- [ ] In-person or virtual interviews are scheduled with the hiring manager.
- [ ] Hiring manager and HR Partner interview candidates.
- [ ] The hiring manager and HR Partner decide if additional interviews are necessary and schedule them as needed.
- [ ] Perform additional testing to check for qualifications.
- [ ] New Hire is selected.
- [ ] If appropriate, send an employee to the drug testing center.
- [ ] Review background, reference, and drug tests for issues.
- [ ] Hiring Manager Approves Hire; if necessary, get senior leadership to approve.
- [ ] Send the offer letter via email, including the employment at will statement.
- [ ] Complete background and reference checks using best practices of the Fair Credit Reporting Act.
  www.ftc.gov/legal-library/browse/statutes/fair-credit-reporting-act
- [ ] Employee accepts the offer.
- [ ] Create an employee personnel file.

Talent Acquisition Checklist

- [ ] Send new employee paperwork to the employee.
- [ ] Notify the state of the new hire.
- [ ] Communicate to IT, Security, Payroll, Operations, Leadership, and other departments of the new hire.
- [ ] Communicate with the other applicants.
- [ ] Schedule the first day of work.
- [ ] Add the employee to the payroll system.
- [ ] Add the employee to the security system.
- [ ] Add the employee to the workers' compensation database.
- [ ] Prep for orientation and onboarding.

Talent Acquisition Checklist

LEGAL CONCERNS

DISCRIMINATION

The user should make sure they know all discrimination laws, particularly Title VII of the 1964 Civil Rights Act, the Americans with Disabilities Act, the Fair Labor Standard Act, the Age Discrimination in Employment Act, and The Pregnancy Act of 1978.

LEGAL QUESTIONS

The user should review what questions are legal and which ones are not.

BACKGROUND CHECKS

Candidates should be notified of any background or credit checks before they happen.

RESOURCES:

How to Conduct a Lawful Interview
smallbusiness.chron.com/conduct-lawful-interview-32282.html

Conducting Remote Interviews Checklist

PURPOSE

Doing interviews remotely can be challenging but not impossible—this *Ultimate HR Checklist* provides tips and practices to ensure a smooth process for the applicant and organization.

DEFINITIONS

Remote Work: In this *Ultimate HR Checklist*, we use the term remote work to mean work from home, work from anywhere, telework, virtual, or hybrid workplace. It is important for organizations to state what their remote work policy is clearly.

FLSA or Fair Labor Standard Act: A federal law that oversees how employees are paid

Employ: By statutory definition, the term "employ" includes "to suffer or permit to work." The workweek ordinarily includes all time during which an employee is required to be on the employer's premises, on duty, or at a prescribed workplace.

"Workday," in general, means the period between the time on any particular day when such employee commences their "principal activity" and the time on that day at which they cease such principal activity or activities; therefore, the workday may be longer than the employee's scheduled shift, hours, a tour of duty, or production line time.

Conducting Remote Interviews Checklist

- [ ] Start with a phone interview to decide if a video interview is necessary.
- [ ] Let the applicant know what to expect with a virtual interview.
- [ ] Verify that they have a webcam or some other video capability.
- [ ] Create an applicant information sheet with suggestions and instructions.
  - Connection instructions
  - Professional attire reminder
  - Who will initiate the video call
  - Phone number to call if there are problems
  - Lighting—have a light behind the camera pointed towards the applicant
  - Microphone—if possible, use an external microphone for better sound
  - Camera—have it horizontal and level at the eyes/face of the applicant
  - Look into the camera when speaking
  - Best to have a quiet and distraction-free area
- [ ] Poor connection? Try shutting off video and continuing with voice only.
- [ ] Be prepared—review the application and resume ahead of time.
- [ ] Use an interview guide with similar questions to ask all candidates.
- [ ] Maintain calm and speak concisely.
- [ ] Build trust with candidates early on by introducing yourself and explaining the process—also thank them for using the video format.
- [ ] Dress professionally or within the appearance standards of your organization.
- [ ] "Wait for a beat" to make sure applicant is finished with their thought.
- [ ] Put extra effort into listening actively to the applicant.
- [ ] Have a neutral background with good lighting.
- [ ] Keep gestures and movement to a minimum to avoid distracting behavior yet still use positive non-verbal cues like smiling often and giving a thumbs-up to show the applicant you are engaged.
- [ ] Avoid looking at your phone or signaling and talking to people off-screen. If necessary, go on mute and pause the video. Apologize to the candidate.
- [ ] Decide if you are going to record the interview and make sure you know the laws regarding consent and informing the candidate.
- [ ] End the discussion on a positive note. Thank the candidate for their time and for engaging in the video interview process.

Conducting Remote Interviews Checklist

LEGAL CONCERNS

DISCRIMINATION

The user should make sure they know all discrimination laws, particularly Title VII of the 1964 Civil Rights Act, Americans with Disabilities Act, Fair Labor Standard Act, Age Discrimination in Employment Act, and The Pregnancy Act of 1978.

LEGAL QUESTIONS

The user should review what questions are legal and which ones are not.

BACKGROUND CHECKS

Candidates should be notified of any background or credit checks before they happen.

RESOURCES

Article: What shouldn't I ask when hiring?
www.eeoc.gov/employers/small-business/what-shouldnt-i-ask-when-hiring

How to Conduct a Lawful Interview
smallbusiness.chron.com/conduct-lawful-interview-32282.html

Video Job Interviews: Legal Issues With Remote Access for Applicants
www.natlawreview.com/article/video-job-interviews-legal-issues-remote-access-applicants

Hiring Process Checklist

PURPOSE

The Hiring Process is one of the most impactful for any organization. This *Ultimate HR Checklist* provides a guide from the beginning to the end of the Recruitment Process, from identifying the need to fill the job and onboarding the employee. Use this to guide and improve your own strategy and ensure that you don't miss any essential steps.

DEFINITIONS

FLSA or Fair Labor Standard Act: A federal law that oversees how employees are paid

Employ: By statutory definition, the term "employ" includes "to suffer or permit to work." The workweek ordinarily includes all time during which an employee is required to be on the employer's premises, on duty, or at a prescribed workplace.

"Workday," in general, means the period between the time on any particular day when such employee commences their "principal activity" and the time on that day at which they cease such principal activity or activities; therefore, the workday may be longer than the employee's scheduled shift, hours, a tour of duty, or production line time.

Hiring Process Checklist

PREP WORK

- ☐ Write Job Description (see Job Description Checklist)
- ☐ Decide on Compensation Package Range
- ☐ Clarify the Fair Labor Standard Act Exemption Status

ADVERTISE THE OPENING

- ☐ Write Appealing Job Posting
- ☐ Include:
  - Accurate job title
  - List of Responsibilities
  - Required Skills
  - Location
  - Salary Range
  - Company Benefits
  - Application Process
  - State Requirements
- ☐ Post Internally
- ☐ Communicate to employees referral bonus opportunity
- ☐ Research the best place to advertise
  - Social Media (Facebook, Instagram, LinkedIn, etc.)
  - Internet Websites (Indeed, Career Builder, Zip Recruiter, Craig's List, etc.)
  - Professional and Industry Organizations
  - Other media (Newspapers, Magazines, Radio, Television, etc.)
  - Temp to Hire
  - Headhunters (Professional Recruiters)
  - Networking
- ☐ Post the Job

RESUME/APPLICATION REVIEW

- [ ] Review resume for grammar or spelling errors
- [ ] Review resume compared to required job knowledge
- [ ] Review resume compared to the required job experience
- [ ] Review resume compared to other resumes
- [ ] Create a list of Yes candidates

INTERVIEW PREP

- [ ] Choose a type of interview (Panel, Group, Serial, One-on-One)
- [ ] Schedule interviews (people, room, date, and time)
- [ ] Pick eight or ten competencies
- [ ] Create five or six questions for each competency
- [ ] Create a simple scorecard for position
- [ ] Develop sample job tests
- [ ] Communicate competencies and questions to interviewers
- [ ] Discuss format with interviewers
- [ ] Provide interviewers Job Description and Resume

PHONE SCREEN INTERVIEW

- [ ] Check for the required certification
- [ ] Ask questions to qualify the individual
- [ ] Provide a detailed explanation of the job

IN-PERSON OR VIRTUAL

- [ ] Introduce yourself and your role
- [ ] Introduce other attendees
- [ ] Provide an overview of the position
- [ ] Ask behavioral or situational questions—allow the candidate to talk 80% of the time
- [ ] Follow-up with curious questions to get more information
- [ ] Have candidate complete any necessary job tests
- [ ] Allow time for the candidate to ask any questions

Hiring Process Checklist

ADDITIONAL INTERVIEWS

- [ ] Schedule with appropriate persons
- [ ] Provide Job Description, Resume, and Scorecard
- [ ] Be communication go-between
- [ ] Follow-up

HIRE DECISIONS

- [ ] Review Job Expectations compare to the candidate
- [ ] Pick the best qualified
- [ ] Check References

OFFER LETTER CONTINGENT ON BACKGROUND CHECKS

- [ ] Title
- [ ] Starting Salary
- [ ] Job Benefits
- [ ] Supervisor Name and Contact Information
- [ ] Employment-at-Will Statement
- [ ] Employee Handbook

BACKGROUND CHECKS

- [ ] Medical Exam
- [ ] Criminal History
- [ ] Credit Report
- [ ] Driving Records
- [ ] Check state regulations about background checks

FINAL AGREEMENT

- [ ] Congrats to Employee
- [ ] Supervisor welcomes new employees
- [ ] Communicate with other applicants about decision
- [ ] Capture Interview notes for documentation

Hiring Process Checklist

LEGAL CONCERNS

DISCRIMINATION

The user should make sure they know all discrimination laws, particularly Title VII of the 1964 Civil Rights Act, Americans with Disabilities Act, Fair Labor Standard Act, Age Discrimination in Employment Act, and The Pregnancy Act of 1978.

LEGAL QUESTIONS

The user should review what questions are legal and which ones are not.

BACKGROUND CHECKS

Candidates should be notified of any background or credit checks before they happen.

RESOURCES

Article: What shouldn't I ask when hiring?
www.eeoc.gov/employers/small-business/what-shouldnt-i-ask-when-hiring

How to Conduct a Lawful Interview
smallbusiness.chron.com/conduct-lawful-interview-32282.html

Interview and Pre-employment Checklist

PURPOSE

"The pre-employment process should be limited to those essential qualifications for determining if a person is qualified to do the job; whereas information regarding race, sex, national origin, age, and religion are irrelevant in such determination." (Prohibited Employment Policies/Practices, 2021)

The interview process can be the biggest legal exposure if done incorrectly and without awareness of lawful questions. This *Ultimate HR Checklist* provides the questions to avoid and questions to ask. Using these questions can keep you safe and legal in the interview and pre-employment process.

DEFINITIONS

Race: Employers should not request information that discloses or tends to reveal an applicant's race unless it has a legitimate business need for such information. (Prohibited Employment Policies/Practices, 2021)

Height & Weight: It is illegal for the most part unless the employer can demonstrate how the need is related to the job.

Financial Information: Federal EEO laws prohibit employers from illegally discriminating when using financial information to make employment decisions.

Background Checks: Background checks are legal, but the candidate must be aware that they will happen and be allowed to defend themselves.

Religious Affiliation or Beliefs: Questions about an applicant's religious affiliation or beliefs (unless the religion is a bona fide occupational qualification (BFOQ)) are generally viewed as non-job-related and problematic under federal law. (Prohibited Employment Policies/Practices, 2021)

Citizenship: Most employers should not ask whether or not a job applicant has citizenship before making an offer of employment. (Prohibited Employment Policies/Practices, 2021)

Marital Status or Number of Children: Questions around marital status and children could violate Title VII and be considered discriminatory.

Gender: Questions around gender, unless a BFOQ, are generally viewed as non-job-related and problematic under Title VII.

Disability: Under the ADA, employers cannot ask disability-related questions or require medical examinations until the candidate has been given a conditional job offer.

Interview and Pre-employment Checklist

POTENTIALLY ILLEGAL INTERVIEW QUESTIONS

TOP 30 QUESTIONS TO AVOID

1. Do you have any children?
2. Do you have a disability or handicap?
3. Do you own or rent a home?
4. What part of town do you live in?
5. What is your marital status?
6. Have you ever had a serious illness?
7. How will your "significant other" feel about the amount of time you will be traveling for this job?
8. What medications are you currently taking?
9. Have you filed any workers' compensation claims?
10. Have any of your close relatives had a heart attack or been diagnosed with a heart condition?
11. Have you had a genetic test to determine whether you are at risk for cancer?
12. Have you ever been arrested?
13. Can you provide us with a recent photograph?
14. What is your birth date? Or How old are you?
15. What is your race?
16. What church do you go to?
17. Are you a citizen of the US?
18. What is your nationality?
19. What language is spoken in your home?
20. What is your religion?
21. To what organization, clubs, societies, and lodges do you belong?
22. What is your height and weight?
23. Do you drive your own car?
24. When did you graduate high school?
25. Do you have a bank account?

Interview and Pre-employment Checklist

26. When did you first start working?
27. Did you receive an honorable discharge from the military?
28. What gender do you identify as?
29. Do you like to drink socially?
30. Did you take any sick days or extended medical leave last year?

Interview and Pre-employment Checklist

TOP 30 QUESTIONS TO ASK

1. What career accomplishments make you proud?
2. Tell me a time when you failed and what you learned from it, and how you got back on track.
3. What makes this job ideal for you?
4. What strengths will you bring to the team, and how do you think they can positively impact the organization?
5. Why are you leaving your current employer?
6. What one professional trait are you working on to improve this year?
7. Tell me what interests you about this company and how it fits your career goals.
8. Tell me a situation where you resolved a disagreement between coworkers.
9. What attributes make a good leader? Good coworker?
10. What is your perfect work environment? Or when are you most productive?
11. Give me an example of when you went above and beyond in your last organization. How did that make you feel?
    What type of recognition did you get?
12. Tell me a time conflict developed with a coworker and how you handled it.
13. Give me an example of how you have dealt with tight deadlines. What was your strategy to accomplish your goals?
14. What holds you back from achieving your goals?
15. What are your professional goals? How does this job fit into them?
16. What three factors motivate you to do a better job?
17. How would others describe your work? How does that differ from how you would describe your work?
18. Tell me, when your boss gave you constructive feedback, and it was wrong, how did you handle it?
19. How have your career goals changed over time?
20. What challenges do you see impacting our industry, and what should the organization be doing to prepare for it?
21. Tell me a time you bent the rules in your last organization to solve an issue.
22. Give me an example of when you influenced your coworkers to go a different direction because you felt it would offer the best solution.

Interview and Pre-employment Checklist

23. How do you prioritize and manage your workload?
24. What isn't on your resume that I should know about you?
25. If you could write your job description, what would it say?
26. Tell me a time you made the wrong decision and how you recover.
27. Describe the best leader you ever worked for or with?
28. How do you build connections on a team?
29. When coworkers are not "pulling their weight," how do you respond?
30. What questions do you have for me?

Interview and Pre-employment Checklist

LEGAL CONCERNS

DISCRIMINATION

The user should make sure they know all discrimination laws, particularly Title VII of the 1964 Civil Rights Act, Americans with Disabilities Act, Fair Labor Standard Act, Age Discrimination in Employment Act, and The Pregnancy Act of 1978.

LEGAL QUESTIONS

The user should review what questions are legal and which ones are not.

BACKGROUND CHECKS

Candidates should be notified of any background or credit checks before they happen.

RESOURCES

Article: What shouldn't I ask when hiring?
www.eeoc.gov/employers/small-business/what-shouldnt-i-ask-when-hiring

How to Conduct a Lawful Interview
smallbusiness.chron.com/conduct-lawful-interview-32282.html

Video Job Interviews: Legal Issues With Remote Access for Applicants
www.natlawreview.com/article/video-job-interviews-legal-issues-remote-access-applicants

New Employee Paperwork

PURPOSE

This *Ultimate HR Checklist* will help you remember all the steps needed in the new hire process. Consistency is "the name of the game" in HR, and being sure to cover all the items in this part of the process is essential.

DEFINITIONS

New Employee: The employee has started with your company for the first time.

Employ: By statutory definition, the term "employ" includes "to suffer or permit to work." The workweek ordinarily includes all time during which an employee is required to be on the employer's premises, on duty, or at a prescribed workplace.

"Workday," in general, means the period between the time on any particular day when such employee commences their "principal activity" and the time on that day at which they cease such principal activity or activities; therefore, the workday may be longer than the employee's scheduled shift, hours, a tour of duty, or production line time.

New Employee Paperwork Checklist

- [ ] Review employee Handbook with employee
- [ ] Have employee acknowledge receipt of the handbook
- [ ] If necessary, complete a confidentiality agreement
- [ ] Complete Form I-9 copy documents
- [ ] Have employee complete W-4
- [ ] File new hire reporting form with the designated state agency
- [ ] If appropriate, have employees sign-up for benefits
- [ ] Capture Employee's Social Security Number
- [ ] Create an Employee Personnel File
- [ ] Create an Employee Confidential/Medical File
- [ ] Direct Deposit Form
- [ ] Personal and Emergency Contact Information
- [ ] Provide Computer/email Log-in information
- [ ] If appropriate, create business cards
- [ ] Receipt of equipment/uniforms issued
- [ ] If necessary, copy the employee's driver's license
- [ ] Be sure to check state regulations for confidentiality and non-compete agreements.

New Employee Paperwork

LEGAL CONCERNS

TITLE VII OF THE CIVIL RIGHTS ACT OF 1964

Title VII prohibits employment discrimination based on race, color, religion, sex, and national origin. All employers in the United States with fifteen or more employees for each working day in each of twenty or more calendar weeks in the current or preceding calendar year.

IMMIGRATION REFORM AND CONTROL ACT OF 1986

Under federal law, employers must verify that all employees are legally authorized to work in the United States of America and keep forms verifying that employees are legally authorized to work in the USA.

IRS: NEW EMPLOYEE DOCUMENTATION

Employers are required to get each employee's name and social security number and enter them on Form W-2. Employers must know how much income tax to withhold from employees' wages. Every employee should complete Form W-4 before they start to work.

RESOURCES

Collecting Information when Hiring Employees
www.irs.gov/businesses/small-businesses-self-employed/hiring-employees

EEO Data Collections
www.eeoc.gov/data/eeo-data-collections

U.S. Citizen and Immigration Services
www.uscis.gov

Offer Letter Checklist

PURPOSE

A well-crafted and comprehensive offer letter is a tangible way to begin an employment relationship. While not legally binding, it does clarify the job offer proposition for the candidate by answering their basic questions, confirming any verbal discussions, providing the candidate with a tangible validation of their opportunity, and building excitement about working for your company.

DEFINITIONS

FLSA STATUS: Fair Labor Standard Act sets regulations on how an employee will be paid either as a Non-Exempt Employee who is eligible for overtime or Exempt employee who is not eligible for overtime.

Pay Period: The period in which the employee is being paid. Please check with your state laws to see what pay requirements there are.

Offer Letter Checklist

- [ ] Name and Address
- [ ] Position/Title
- [ ] Department
- [ ] FLSA classification—Exempt/Salaried or Non-Exempt/Hourly
- [ ] Status—Full Time or Part-Time
- [ ] Start Date
- [ ] Where and when to report on the first day
- [ ] Manager's name
- [ ] Manager's title
- [ ] Pay period—weekly/bi-weekly/monthly
- [ ] Base salary or pay rate
- [ ] Bonuses or Commissions eligibility information
- [ ] If Exempt/Salaried—yearly salary is also noted in per pay period terms ($[salary] annualized, paid at a weekly rate of $[salary/52]).
- [ ] Sign-on bonus
- [ ] Vacation/Sick Time/ Personal Time Off Policy
- [ ] Automobile Allowance
- [ ] Relocation information (might be a separate agreement)
- [ ] Benefits information
- [ ] The clause at the end of the offer letter explaining that it is not a contract and that employment is still at-will
- [ ] Disclaimer statement that this offer is contingent upon the successful completion of a background check, pre-employment drug screening, and review business references
- [ ] Location for a candidate to sign
- [ ] HR representative signature at the bottom

Offer Letter Checklist

LEGAL CONCERNS

TITLE VII OF THE CIVIL RIGHTS ACT OF 1964

Title VII prohibits employment discrimination based on race, color, religion, sex, and national origin. All employers in the United States with fifteen or more employees for each working day in each of twenty or more calendar weeks in the current or preceding calendar year.

IMMIGRATION REFORM AND CONTROL ACT OF 1986

Under federal law, employers must verify that all employees are legally authorized to work in the United States of America and keep forms verifying that employees are legally authorized to work in the USA.

OFFER LETTER

The offer letter is a simple document providing the employee with information about their employment. The employer must be careful not to create a binding agreement with the offer letter as this may reduce the role of Employment-at-Will. The employer should also not use discriminatory language or phrases within the documentation.

RESOURCES

7 Things to Include in Every Employment Offer Letter
www.innovativeemployeesolutions.com/blog/6-things-include-every-employment-offer-letter

10 Things To Double Check On An Offer Letter
www.glassdoor.com/blog/how-to-read-offer-letter

Onboarding Checklist

PURPOSE

Welcoming new employees with a robust onboarding process can help improve the new hire retention rate. The initial impression a new hire has and their first few days, weeks, and months can determine if they will stay or decide they are in the wrong company. This *Ultimate HR Checklist* can help you to ensure new employees have all the necessary tools, resources, support, and knowledge to become successful and highly productive at your organization.

Onboarding Checklist

- [ ] Create a welcome atmosphere during the interview
- [ ] Communicate Job Offer
- [ ] Accepts Offer
- [ ] The manager sends a welcoming note
- [ ] Human Resources sends a welcoming gift
- [ ] Send Employee Package
  - Employee Handbook
  - New Employee Paperwork Requirements
  – New Employee Guide
  – Parking Location
  – Lunch
  – Dress code
  – Security Information
  – Employee Entrance
  – Break Information
  – Coworkers
  - Organizational Structure
  - First Day Expectations
- [ ] Prepare For New Employee
  - Set-up Computer
  - Set-up Desk Phone
  - Set-up Mobile Phone
  - Prepare Workstation
  - Security Clearance/Employee Identification
  - Set-up Email Address
  - If applicable, order business cards
  - Set-up direct deposit
- [ ] Communicate to necessary departments and coworkers
  - Human Resources
  - Payroll
  - Security
  - Operations
  - Senior Management
  - Others

Onboarding Checklist

- ☐ Create an Onboarding Plan
    - Schedule meetings with appropriate staff
    - Schedule Training/Orientation
    - Prepare New Employee Paperwork
- ☐ First Day
    - The manager meets Employee at Entrance
    - Review New Employee Paperwork
    - Review Organization's Mission and Vision
    - Discuss with Employee
  - Company Policies
  - Attendance Policies
  - Introductory Period
  - Time Cards
  - Work Schedule
    - Review of Employee Handbook
    - Manager reviews Job Description with Employee
    - Introductions to coworkers and senior management
    - Tour of Facility
  - Bathroom
  - Break Room/Lunch Room
  - Parking
  - Departments
  - Evacuation Plan
    - Review of Safety Information
    - Have a Celebration Lunch/Introduction Party
- ☐ Assign employee a mentor or partner

Onboarding Checklist

☐ First Month
- Set Employee Expectations
  – Results
  – Tasks and Responsibility
  – Behavioral Norms
- Organizational Training
  – Safety
  – Ethical
  – Anti-harassment
  – Anti-discrimination
  – Vision and Mission
  – History
  – Long Term Goals
- Departmental Training
- Equipment
- Tools
- Expectations
- Process/Procedures

Onboarding Checklist

LEGAL CONCERNS

TITLE VII OF THE CIVIL RIGHTS ACT OF 1964

Title VII prohibits employment discrimination based on race, color, religion, sex, and national origin. All employers in the United States with fifteen or more employees for each working day in each of twenty or more calendar weeks in the current or preceding calendar year.

IMMIGRATION REFORM AND CONTROL ACT OF 1986

Under federal law, employers must verify that all employees are legally authorized to work in the United States of America and keep forms verifying that employees are legally authorized to work in the USA.

RESOURCES

Indeed.com—Onboarding Best Practices
www.indeed.com/hire/c/info/onboarding-best-practices

SHRM.com—New Employee Onboarding Guide
www.shrm.org/resourcesandtools/hr-topics/talent-acquisition/pages/new-employee-onboarding-guide.aspx

Simple Interview Scorecard

PURPOSE

To help keep interviews on track with candidates, an Interview Scorecard is helpful. This simple tool can help keep the discussion productive and ensure the interviewer collects the details they need to make an informed decision about the candidate. The Interview Scorecard from *Ultimate HR Checklists* will also help keep the interview process consistent and allow interviewers to remember candidates when conducting multiple interviews.

TITLE OF POSITION:

HIRING MANAGER:

ESSENTIAL FUNCTIONS OF JOB:

DATE:

SCALE	
1	NEEDS IMPROVEMENT
2	SLIGHTLY NEEDS IMPROVEMENT
3	MEETS
4	SLIGHTLY EXCEEDS
5	EXCEEDS

Simple Interview Scorecard

COMPETENCIES									
CANDIDATES	ONE	TWO	THREE	FOUR	FIVE	SIX	SEVEN	TOTAL	NOTES

Simple Interview Scorecard

Values Diversity	Motivating Others	Adaptability/Flexibility
Confident	Organizational Awareness	Ambition
Gracious	Performance Management	Building Relationships
Technical Expertise	Persuasion	Caution
Emotional Intelligence	Planning And Organizing	Communication
Visionary	Presentation	Conflict Resolution
Service Oriented	Prioritization	Creativity
Disciplined	Project Management	Innovation
Committed	Problem Solving	Customer Orientation
Accountable	Gratitude	Decision Making
Humble	Resilience	Delegation
Decisive	Sales	Detail Orientation
Driven/Passionate	Self-Improvement	Employee Development
Connected	Self-Awareness	Initiative
Influencer	Setting Goals	Integrity
Courageous	Strategic Thinking	Judgment
Risk Taker	Teamwork	Leadership Skills
Open To Learn	Time Management	Proactive Skills

Simple Interview Scorecard

LEGAL CONCERNS

When using a scorecard, be careful that if you decide to hire a person who is not the best on paper, i.e., has the highest scores, the reason is not discriminatory. For instance, you won't hire them because they are too old, or the wrong religion. We strongly urge you to make sure you hire the person with the highest score to reduce the risk of discriminatory practices.

TITLE VII OF THE CIVIL RIGHTS ACT OF 1964

> Title VII prohibits employment discrimination based on race, color, religion, sex, and national origin. All employers in the United States with fifteen or more employees for each working day in each of twenty or more calendar weeks in the current or preceding calendar year.

RESOURCES

Shareables.com—Tips on how to use job interview scorecards
> hires.shareable.com/blog/job-interview-scorecards

Harvard Business Review—A Scorecard for Making Better Hiring Decisions
> hbr.org/2016/02/a-scorecard-for-making-better-hiring-decisions

Hiring Independent Contractors

Independent Contractors Checklist

PURPOSE

Federal, State, and Local authorities want to make sure any worker an employer has hired is appropriately classified. There are four classifications: volunteer (not allowed with private employers), statutory employees, common-law employees, and independent contractors. This *Ultimate HR Checklist* provides a good roadmap to ensure employers are compliant with federal laws and regulations.

DEFINITIONS

Employ: By statutory definition, the term "employ" includes "to suffer or permit to work." The workweek ordinarily includes all time when an employee is required to be on the employer's premises, on duty, or at a prescribed workplace.

"Workday," in general, means the period between the time on any particular day when such employee commences their "principal activity" and the time on that day at which they cease such principal activity or activities; therefore, the workday may be longer than the employee's scheduled shift, hours, a tour of duty, or production line time.

Independent Contractor Checklist

- [ ] Describe the work that needs to be done
    - Expected Outcomes
    - Deadlines
    - Location of Work
    - Tools or Equipment Needed
    - Processes to be followed
- [ ] Employee versus independent contractor
    - Expected Outcomes
    - Deadlines
    - Location of Work
    - Tools or Equipment Needed
    - Processes to be followed
- [ ] Review the IRS 20 Factor Test
- [ ] Review the ABC Test
- [ ] Review the Department of Labor Economic Reality Test
- [ ] Decide if they are an Independent Contractor
    - (If not—go to hiring employees)
- [ ] Verify References from past clients
- [ ] Review Website and other social media information
- [ ] Negotiate Responsibilities and Rates
- [ ] Capture contact Information
- [ ] Write Contract
    - Terms
    - Responsibilities and Deliverables
    - Payment-Related Details
    - Confidentiality Clause
    - Contract Termination
    - Choice of Law
    - Ethical Considerations
- [ ] Review contract with Accounts Payable/Legal/Leadership Team

Independent Contractor Checklist

- ☐ Have contract signed by Independent Contractor
- ☐ Independent Contractor Completes W-9
- ☐ Ask for a copy of Liability Insurance
- ☐ Ask for a copy of worker's compensation Insurance
- ☐ Ask for a copy of their Business License if necessary
- ☐ Proof of independent Business location (even if home-based)
- ☐ If applicable, ask for Safety Training Certification

Independent Contractor Checklist

LEGAL CONCERNS

FAIR LABOR STANDARD ACT (FLSA)

Created in 1938, the Fair Labor Standard Acts sets the policies we use today to set proper compensation for our employees, including the federal minimum wage, the standard salary level, child labor laws, what is considered hours worked, correct record keeping, and the difference between those employees who receive overtime and those that do not.

STATE AND LOCAL LAWS

Each State has its own ABC tests to see if an individual qualifies as an employee or an independent contractor.

TAX LAW

One of the main reasons the government wants to make sure that you classify your employees correctly is to ensure the proper amount of taxes is given to the government.

WORKER'S COMPENSATION

Worker's Compensation Insurance is used for employees only. Your Worker's compensation insurance company will want to make sure you classify your workers correctly, so they don't have any hidden costs.

RESOURCES

DOL.gov—Fact Sheet 13: Employment Relationship Under the Fair Labor Standards Act (FLSA)
www.dol.gov/agencies/whd/fact-sheets/13-flsa-employment-relationship

Misclassification of Employees as Independent Contractors
www.dol.gov/agencies/whd/flsa/misclassification

Independent Contractor Status Under the Fair Labor Standards Act (FLSA): Withdrawal
www.federalregister.gov/documents/2021/05/06/2021-09518/independent-contractor-status-under-the-fair-labor-standards-act-flsa-withdrawal

IRS 20 Factor Checklist

PURPOSE

This *Ultimate HR Checklist* provides the actual IRS 20 Factors used to determine whether an employer-employee relationship exists. It was developed in 1987, based on examining IRS cases and rulings. It looks at the degree of importance of various factors depending on the occupation and the factual context in which the services are performed. According to the United States Supreme Court, bright-line determines whether a worker is an employee or an independent contractor. We use the IRS 20 Factor test to better understand and reduce risk to our organization.

DEFINITIONS

Employ: By statutory definition, the term "employ" includes "to suffer or permit to work." The workweek ordinarily includes all time when an employee is required to be on the employer's premises, on duty, or at a prescribed workplace.

"Workday," in general, means the period between the time on any particular day when such employee commences their "principal activity" and the time on that day at which they cease such principal activity or activities; therefore, the workday may be longer than the employee's scheduled shift, hours, tour of duty, or production line time.

IRS 20 Factor Checklist

		QUESTIONS	YES/NO
1	Level of Instruction	Does the employer direct or control when, where, and how work is to be done?	
2	Amount of Training	Do you require the worker to take company training?	
3	Degree Business Integration	Are the functions the worker does essential to your business?	
4	The extent of Personal Services	Do you insist that the worker complete the work themselves?	
5	Control of Assistants	Do you retain control of who assists the worker in completing the project stated in the contract?	
6	Continuity of Relationship	Is there a continuing relationship between your company and the Worker?	
7	Flexibility of Schedule	Do you dictate the hours the worker must work?	
8	Demands for Full-time Work	Do you require the worker to work a full-time schedule with your company?	
9	Need for On-site Services	Is the work performed required to be done on company property?	
10	Sequence of Work	Do you require the worker to follow a set process when completing the work?	
11	Requirements for Reports	Is the worker required to send in regular reports?	
12	Method of Payment	Is the Worker paid by the hour, week, or month?	
13	Payment of Business and Travel Expenses	Do you directly reimburse the Worker for business/travel expenses?	
14	Provision of Tools and Materials	Does the business provide the tools and equipment necessary to do the job?	
15	Investment in Facilities	Have you made a significant investment in facilities used by the Worker to perform services?	
16	Realization of Profit or Loss	Does the worker have an opportunity for profit and loss based on their decisions?	

IRS 20 Factor Checklist

		QUESTIONS	YES/NO
17	Work for Multiple Companies	Does the Worker only perform services for your company?	
18	Availability to Public	Do you limit the number of clients a worker can have?	
19	Control over Discharge	Does your company have the right to discharge the Worker?	
20	Right of Termination	Does the worker have the right to terminate their services at any time?	

NOTES

If the answer is yes—it is more likely the individual should be an employee of your company. There are no clear guidelines of a particular number of questions answered yes to make an individual an employee; however, the more yes you have, the more likely the work is an employee.

Check out the ABC Test and the DOL of Labor Economic Reality Test to clarify whether the worker is an employee or an independent contractor.

IRS 20 Factor Checklist

LEGAL CONCERNS

FAIR LABOR STANDARD ACT (FLSA)

Created in 1938, the Fair Labor Standard Acts sets the policies we use today to set proper compensation for our employees, including the federal minimum wage, the standard salary level, child labor laws, what is considered hours worked, correct record keeping, and the difference between those employees who receive overtime and those that do not.

STATE AND LOCAL LAWS

Each State has its own ABC tests to see if an individual qualifies as an employee or an independent contractor.

TAX LAW

One of the main reasons the government wants to make sure that you classify your employees correctly is to ensure the proper amount of taxes is given to the government.

WORKER'S COMPENSATION

Worker's Compensation Insurance is used for employees only. Your Worker's compensation insurance company will want to make sure you classify your workers correctly, so they don't have any hidden costs.

RESOURCES

DOL.gov—Fact Sheet 13: Employment Relationship Under the Fair Labor Standards Act (FLSA)
www.dol.gov/agencies/whd/fact-sheets/13-flsa-employment-relationship

Misclassification of Employees as Independent Contractors
www.dol.gov/agencies/whd/flsa/misclassification

Independent Contractor Status Under the Fair Labor Standards Act (FLSA): Withdrawal
www.federalregister.gov/documents/2021/05/06/2021-09518/independent-contractor-status-under-the-fair-labor-standards-act-flsa-withdrawal

IRS.gov—Independent Contractor (Self-Employed) or Employee?
www.irs.gov/businesses/small-businesses-self-employed/independent-contractor-self-employed-or-employee

ABC Three-Factor Test Checklist

PURPOSE

There are several "tests" to determine if an individual is an employee or independent contractor. The ABC test is performed to determine if a worker is an independent contractor. An employer must answer yes to all three parts of the test to qualify a worker as a contractor. The IRS automatically categorizes workers as employees unless proven otherwise.

Please note that each state's ABC Test may vary.

DEFINITIONS

ABC Test: A legal test used by states to determine whether a worker is an employee or an independent contractor.

ABC Three Factor Test Checklist

A

The worker's activities are not directed or controlled when performing the work, both under the contract for providing the services and in reality.

- [ ] Do you perform training for the worker?
- [ ] Do you provide detailed explanation on how to do the work?
- [ ] Is this worker overseen by a supervisor?
- [ ] Do you provide tools or equipment so the individual can do their job?
- [ ] Is the worker expected to follow a schedule set by the employer?
- [ ] Is the worker liable for their work?
- [ ] If applicable, is the worker responsible for maintaining their license?
- [ ] Does the company set the rate of pay?
- [ ] Is the worker paid on a salary, hour by hour, or as a project?

B

The service provided by the individual is not to be within the usual course of business of the employer or is performed outside all the employer's places of business.

- [ ] Is the work or service part of your essential business?
- [ ] Is the work or services performed at your place of business?

ABC Three Factor Test Checklist

C

The worker is customarily engaged in an independently established trade, occupation, profession, or business of the exact nature of the service performed.

- [ ] Does the worker possess a state license or specialized skills?
- [ ] Does the worker hold themself out as an independent business through business cards, printed invoices, or advertising?
- [ ] Does the worker have a company separate from that of the potential employer?
- [ ] Does the individual have capital investment in the independent company, such as vehicles and equipment?
- [ ] Is the worker required to have their liability insurance, showing that they manage their own risk?
- [ ] Does the worker perform services on their/ own name instead of the potential employer's name?
- [ ] Does the employer use other subcontractors as well? Do they perform similar services?
- [ ] Does the worker have a saleable business or going concern with the existence of an established clientele?
- [ ] Does the worker provide services for more than one entity?
- [ ] Does the performance of services affect the goodwill of the worker rather than the employer?

ABC Three Factor Test Checklist

LEGAL CONCERNS

FAIR LABOR STANDARD ACT (FLSA)

Created in 1938, the Fair Labor Standard Acts sets the policies we use today to set proper compensation for our employees, including the federal minimum wage, the standard salary level, child labor laws, what is considered hours worked, correct record keeping, and the difference between those employees who receive overtime and those that do not.

RESOURCES

What is the ABC Test?
www.thebalancesmb.com/what-is-the-abc-test-for-independent-contractors-4586615

Independent Contractors Checklist (page 108)

DOL Economic Reality Test

PURPOSE

There are several tests to determine if an individual is an employee or independent contractor. The Department of Labor created the "economic reality" test to determine a worker's status as an FLSA employee or an independent contractor. "The test considers whether a worker is in business for themselves (independent contractor) or is economically dependent on a putative employer for work (employee)."

DEFINITIONS

Employ: By statutory definition, the term "employ" includes "to suffer or permit to work." The workweek ordinarily includes all time during which an employee is necessarily required to be on the employer's premises, on duty, or at a prescribed workplace.

"Workday," in general, means the period between the time on any particular day when such employee commences their "principal activity" and the time on that day at which they cease such principal activity or activities; therefore, the workday may be longer than the employee's scheduled shift, hours, tour of duty, or production line time.

DOL Economic Reality Test

If you answer yes to most of these questions, the worker is most likely an independent contractor; otherwise, they are an employee and need to be paid as such. Also, check out the IRS 20 Factor Test and the ABC Test for clarification.

QUALIFICATION	YES/NO
Does the worker have their own business?	
Does the worker control the day-to-day operations of the work?	
Does the worker have an opportunity for profit and loss based on quantity and quality?	
Are there high-level skills required to do the job?	
Is there a sense of impermanence in the working relationship between employer and worker?	
Is the work auxiliary to the essential functions of the business?	

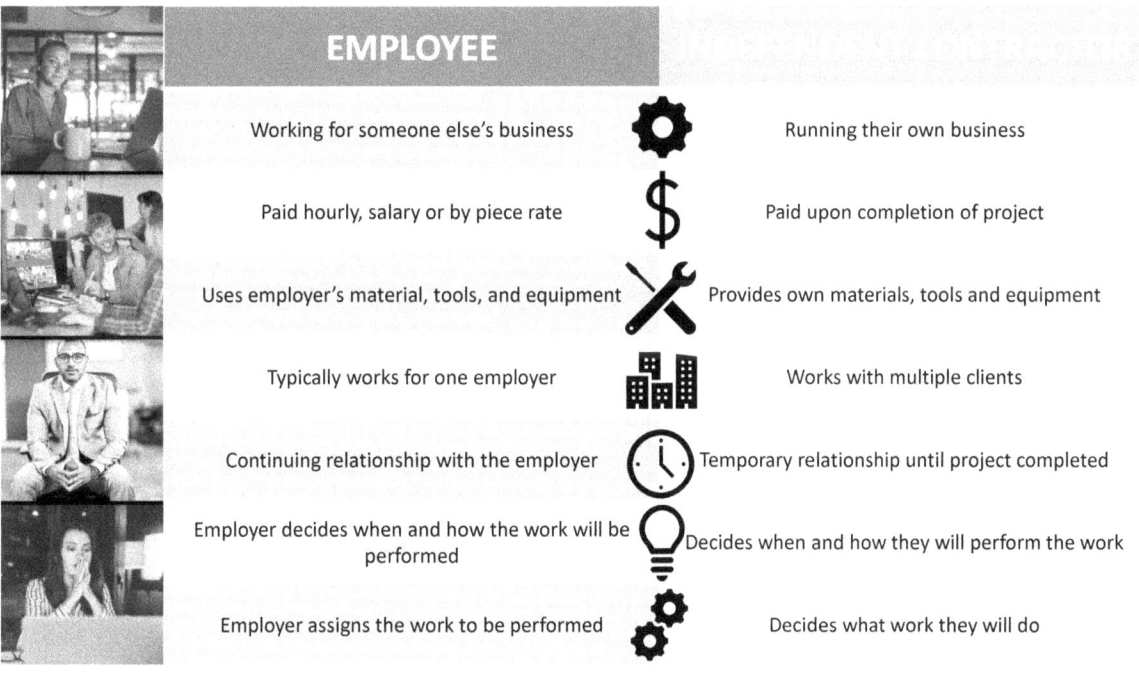

Resourced from the DOL.

DOL Economic Reality Test

LEGAL CONCERNS

FAIR LABOR STANDARD ACT (FLSA)

Created in 1938, the Fair Labor Standard Acts sets the policies we use today to set proper compensation for our employees, including the federal minimum wage, the standard salary level, child labor laws, what is considered hours worked, correct record keeping, and the difference between those employees who receive overtime and those that do not.

STATE AND LOCAL LAWS

Each State has its own ABC tests to see if an individual qualifies as an employee or an independent contractor.

RESOURCES

DOL.gov—Fact Sheet 13: Employment Relationship Under the Fair Labor Standards Act (FLSA)
www.dol.gov/agencies/whd/fact-sheets/13-flsa-employment-relationship

Misclassification of Employees as Independent Contractors
www.dol.gov/agencies/whd/flsa/misclassification
www.dol.gov/agencies/whd/flsa/misclassification/rulemaking

Independent Contractor Status Under the Fair Labor Standards Act (FLSA): Withdrawal
www.federalregister.gov/documents/2021/05/06/2021-09518/independent-contractor-status-under-the-fair-labor-standards-act-flsa-withdrawal

Rewarding Employees (Pay & Benefits)

Calculating Employee Pay Checklist

PURPOSE

Would you work without being paid? Your employees give their efforts in return for being paid. It is the employer's responsibility to make sure they are aligning their pay practices with federal, state, and local laws. *This Ultimate HR Checklist* will help you evaluate and correct your current pay practices.

DEFINITIONS

Pay: Money or funds provided to an individual for work rendered.

Employ: By statutory definition, the term "employ" includes "to suffer or permit to work." The workweek ordinarily includes all time during which an employee is necessarily required to be on the employer's premises, on duty, or at a prescribed workplace.

"Workday," in general, means the period between the time on any particular day when such employee commences their "principal activity" and the time on that day at which they cease such principal activity or activities; therefore, the workday may be longer than the employee's scheduled shift, hours, tour of duty, or production line time.

FLSA: The Fair Labor Standards Act (FLSA) establishes minimum wage, overtime pay, record keeping, and youth employment standards affecting employees in the private sector and Federal, State, and local governments. Covered nonexempt workers are entitled to a minimum wage of not less than $7.25 per hour effective July 24, 2009. Overtime pay at a rate not less than one and one-half times the regular rate of pay is required after 40 hours of work in a workweek.

Non-Exempt Employees: Non-Exempt Employees are employees who are eligible for overtime.

Exempt Employees: Exempt Employees are not eligible for overtime.

Calculating Employee Pay Checklist

☐ Determine if the candidate will be an employee. Check out the HIRING INDEPENDENT CONTRACTORS chapter for more information

- Answer yes to any of the following questions, and the candidate will be an employee:
— Will the company control where, when, what, and how the work is done?
— Will the company be held responsible for the employee's business decisions?
— Will the duties be an essential part of the company's business?

☐ Designate employee's FLSA status

- Exempt: They are exempt if you answer yes to all of the following questions:
— Are they paid a predetermined and fixed salary not subject to reduction because of variations in the quality or quantity of work performed?
— Are they paid more than the adequate minimum standard salary level in your legal jurisdiction?
— Do they pass the "duties" test for the Fair Labor Standards Act overtime exemptions?
- Non-Exempt: They are non-exempt if you answer no to any of the above questions.

☐ Determine starting salary using www.onetonline.org

☐ For non-exempt employees, capture hours worked with a time clock.

☐ If a non-exempt employee works more than 40 hours in one week, give them overtime pay based on 1.5 times their regular rate. *Note: State laws vary on how overtime should be calculated.*

☐ If a non-exempt employee is provided additional enumeration, use it to calculate the regular rate for overtime pay.

Calculating Employee Pay Checklist

LEGAL CONCERNS

FAIR LABOR STANDARD ACT (FLSA)

Created in 1938, the Fair Labor Standard Acts sets the policies we use today to set proper compensation for our employees, including the federal minimum wage, the standard salary level, child labor laws, what is considered hours worked, correct record keeping, and the difference between those employees who receive overtime and those that do not.

RESOURCES

DOL.gov—Wages and the Fair Labor Standards Act
www.dol.gov/agencies/whd/flsa

Fair Labor Standards Act (FLSA) Minimum Wage Poster
www.dol.gov/agencies/whd/posters/flsa

DOL.gov—Handy Reference Guide to the Fair Labor Standards Act
www.dol.gov/agencies/whd/compliance-assistance/handy-reference-guide-flsa

Exempt Status Checklist

PURPOSE

Would you work without being paid? Your employees give their efforts in return for being paid. It is the employer's responsibility to make sure they are aligning their pay practices with federal, state, and local laws. *This Ultimate HR Checklist* will help you evaluate and correct your current pay practices. One of the essential distinctions in employment law is knowing the difference between non-exempt and exempt. This checklist will make sure you are classifying the employee correctly.

DEFINITIONS

Pay: Money or funds provided to an individual for work rendered.

Employ: By statutory definition, the term "employ" includes "to suffer or permit to work." The workweek ordinarily includes all time during which an employee is necessarily required to be on the employer's premises, on duty, or at a prescribed workplace.

"Workday," in general, means the period between the time on any particular day when such employee commences their "principal activity" and the time on that day at which they cease such principal activity or activities; therefore, the workday may be longer than the employee's scheduled shift, hours, tour of duty, or production line time.

FLSA: The Fair Labor Standards Act (FLSA) establishes minimum wage, overtime pay, record keeping, and youth employment standards affecting employees in the private sector and Federal, State, and local governments. Covered nonexempt workers are entitled to a minimum wage of not less than $7.25 per hour effective July 24, 2009. Overtime pay at a rate not less than one and one-half times the regular rate of pay is required after 40 hours of work in a workweek.

Non-Exempt Employees: Non-Exempt Employees are employees who are eligible for overtime.

Exempt Employees: Exempt Employees are not eligible for overtime.

Standard Salary Level: The Department of Labor regulations require executive, administrative, and professional (EAP) employees to be paid at least a minimum salary amount to be exempt from the Fair Labor Standards Act's minimum wage and overtime requirements under section 13(a)(1). For more information check out the DOL website at https://www.dol.gov/agencies/whd/overtime/salary-levels

EXEMPT STATUS CHECKLIST

NONEXEMPT VERSUS EXEMPT EMPLOYEE CHECKLIST

☐ Assume that all non-exempt employees are required to be paid a minimum wage and overtime after 40 hours;

☐ Apply the following three criterion tests based on the FLSA Fact Sheet #17a
   www.dol.gov/sites/dolgov/files/WHD/legacy/files/fs17a_overview.pdf;

☐ Check to see if the employee is compensated on a salary basis above the Standard Salary Level as defined on page 127;

☐ Confirm that they regularly receive a predetermined amount of pay constituting all or part of the employee's salary, which is not subject to reduction because of variation in the quality and quantity of work performed (In other words, are they paid the same amount each pay period?);

☐ Pull up their job description and review it to see if they meet the individual exemptions' duties test;

☐ Remember to check state and local laws on handling overtime. Some states and localities calculate overtime on a daily and weekly basis.

EXECUTIVE EXEMPTION:

All of the following tests must be met:

☐ Check to see if the employee is compensated on a salary basis above the Standard Salary Level as defined on page 127 (Please note that it is the Federal Level, and your state level may vary.);

☐ The employee's primary duty must be managing the enterprise or managing a customarily recognized department or subdivision of the enterprise;

☐ The employee must customarily and regularly direct the work of at least two or more other full-time employees or their equivalent; and

☐ The employee must have the authority to hire or fire other employees, or the employee's suggestions and recommendations as to the hiring, firing, advancement, promotion or any other changes of status of other employees must be given particular weight.

ADMINISTRATIVE EXEMPTIONS:

To qualify for the administrative employee exemption, all of the following tests must be met:

☐ Check to see if the employee is compensated on a salary basis above the Standard Salary Level as defined on page 127;

☐ The employee's primary duty must be the performance of office or non-manual work directly related to the management or general business operations of the employer or the employer's customers; and

☐ The employee's primary duty includes the exercise of discretion and independent judgment concerning matters of significance.

PROFESSIONAL EXEMPTION:

To qualify for the learned professional employee exemption, all of the following tests must be met:

- [ ] Check to see if the employee is compensated on a salary basis above the Standard Salary Level as defined on page 127;
- [ ] The employee's primary duty must be the performance of work requiring advanced knowledge, defined as work which is predominantly intellectual in character and which includes work requiring the regular exercise of discretion and judgment;
- [ ] The advanced knowledge must be in a field of science or learning; and
- [ ] The advanced knowledge must be customarily acquired by a prolonged course of specialized intellectual instruction.

To qualify for the creative professional employee exemption, all of the following tests must be met:

- [ ] Check to see if the employee is compensated on a salary basis above the Standard Salary Level as defined on page 127;
- [ ] The employee's primary duty must be the performance of work requiring invention,

Imagination, originality, or talent in a recognized field of artistic or creative endeavor.

COMPUTER EMPLOYEE EXEMPTION:

To qualify for the computer employee exemption, all of the following tests must be met:

- [ ] Check to see if the employee is compensated on a salary basis above the Standard Salary Level as defined on page 127;
- [ ] The employee must be employed as a computer systems analyst, computer programmer, software engineer, or other similarly skilled worker in the computer field performing the duties described below;

The employee's primary duty must consist of:

1. The application of systems analysis techniques and procedures, including consulting with users, to determine hardware, software, or system functional specifications;

2. The design, development, documentation, analysis, creation, testing, or modification of computer systems or programs, including prototypes, based on and related to the user or system design specifications;

3. The design, documentation, testing, creation, or modification of computer programs related to machine operating systems; or

4. A combination of the duties above, the performance of which requires the same level of skills

Exempt Status Checklist

OUTSIDE SALES EXEMPTION:

To qualify for the outside sales employee exemption, all of the following tests must be met:

☐ The employee's primary duty must be making sales (as defined in the **FLSA**), or obtaining orders or contracts for services or for the use of facilities for which the client or customer will pay a consideration; and

☐ The employee must be customarily and regularly engaged away from the employer's place or places of business.

Exempt Status Checklist

LEGAL CONCERNS

FAIR LABOR STANDARD ACT (FLSA)

Created in 1938, the Fair Labor Standard Acts sets the policies we use today to set proper compensation for our employees, including the federal minimum wage, the standard salary level, child labor laws, what is considered hours worked, correct record keeping, and the difference between those employees who receive overtime and those that do not.

RESOURCES

DOL.gov—Wages and the Fair Labor Standards Act
www.dol.gov/agencies/whd/flsa

Fair Labor Standards Act (FLSA) Minimum Wage Poster
www.dol.gov/agencies/whd/posters/flsa

DOL.gov—Handy Reference Guide to the Fair Labor Standards Act
www.dol.gov/agencies/whd/compliance-assistance/handy-reference-guide-flsa

Benefits Administration Responsibilities Checklist

PURPOSE

HR Departments have many moving parts. The Benefits function is especially sensitive to a large number of considerations and compliance. This *Ultimate HR Checklist* covers some of the primary responsibilities you have when overseeing the benefits function.

DEFINITIONS

Fiduciary: A fiduciary is a person who acts on behalf of the employer, putting the employer's interest ahead of their own with a duty to preserve good faith and trust.

Applicable Larger Employer (ALE): Any company or organization with an average of at least 50 full-time employees. According to the ACA, a full-time employee is someone who works at least 30 hours a week.

Affordable Care Act: The Affordable Care Act, or health care law, contains benefits and responsibilities for employers. The size and structure of your workforce determines what applies to you. An employer's size is determined by the number of its full-time employees, including full-time equivalents.

Benefits Administration Responsibilities Checklist

- [ ] Understand your fiduciary responsibility and that participants receive promised benefits and their rights are not violated.
- [ ] Report and disclose information on benefit plans to participants and governing agencies as required.
- [ ] Determines whether or not your Company is an Applicable Large Employer (ALE) and elects to offer coverage or pay fines accordingly (ALE if average 50+ FT or full-time equivalent employees during the prior calendar year).
- [ ] Maintain evidence of plan's compliance with the Affordable Care Act and following all applicable requirements.
- [ ] Perform regular plan audits to ensure everything is running smoothly and that all financial information is kept accurately.
- [ ] Monitor industry trends to identify ways to serve the company and employees better.
- [ ] Maintain a Summary Plan Description (SPD) Wrap and be prepared to provide it within 30 days after receiving a request.
- [ ] Collaborate with Accounting Department to ensure timely payments of monthly premiums.
- [ ] Audit your benefit invoices every month to ensure you are not paying premiums for former employees (or other ineligible individuals).
- [ ] Ensure employee records with all relevant information (marital status, years of service, hours worked, etc.) are correct and up to date.
- [ ] Research employee satisfaction and respond accordingly based on the results.
- [ ] Maintain clearly defined employment categories for full-time (FT), part-time (PT), temporary and seasonal employees and ensure eligibility guidelines are upheld.
- [ ] Maintain a COBRA administration policy and procedures or outsource COBRA administration to ensure all rights and responsibilities are met.
- [ ] Maintain a HIPAA policy defining permitted use and disclosure of Protected Health Information (PHI).
- [ ] Maintain privacy safeguards in storing and transmitting Protected Health Information (PHI) data, both physical and electronic information.
- [ ] Serve as the primary point of contact for both employees and benefits vendors.

Benefits Administration Responsibilities Checklist

LEGAL CONCERNS

AFFORDABLE CARE ACT

The "Affordable Care Act" (ACA) is the name for the comprehensive health care reform law and its amendments. The law addresses health insurance coverage, health care costs, and preventive care. The law was enacted in two parts: The Patient Protection and Affordable Care Act was signed into law on March 23, 2010, and was amended by the Health Care and Education Reconciliation Act on March 30, 2010.

HIPAA

The Health Insurance Portability and Accountability Act of 1996 (HIPAA) is a federal law that requires the creation of national standards to protect sensitive patient health information from being disclosed without the patient's consent or knowledge.

COBRA

The Consolidated Omnibus Budget Reconciliation Act (COBRA) gives workers and their families who lose their health benefits the right to choose to continue group health benefits provided by their group health plan for limited periods under certain circumstances such as voluntary or involuntary job loss, reduction in the hours worked, the transition between jobs, death, divorce, and other life events. Qualified individuals may be required to pay the entire premium for coverage up to 102% of the cost to the plan.

RESOURCES

HHS.gov—Healthcare
www.hhs.gov/healthcare/index.html

IRS.gov—Affordable Care Act Tax Provisions for Employers
www.irs.gov/affordable-care-act/employers

CDC.gov—HIPAA
www.cdc.gov/phlp/publications/topic/hipaa.html

DOL.gov—Continuation of Health Coverage (COBRA)
www.dol.gov/general/topic/health-plans/cobra

Benefits Disclosures and Notifications Checklist

PURPOSE

If your company or organization is offering medical insurance, many disclosures or notifications could apply to you. This *Ultimate HR Checklist* covers some of the common disclosures and reports you need to know when overseeing the benefits function. If you are unsure of what these items are, contact your Benefits Broker, Consultant, or Attorney.

DEFINITIONS

CHIP: The Children's Health Insurance Program (CHIP) is a joint federal and state program that provides health coverage to uninsured children in families with incomes too high to qualify for Medicaid, but too low to afford private coverage.

FMLA: Family Medical Leave Act

HIPAA: Health Insurance Portability & Accountability Act is a federal law that required the creation of national standards to protect sensitive patient health information from being disclosed without the patient's consent or knowledge.

COBRA: The Consolidated Omnibus Budget Reconciliation Act (COBRA) health benefit provisions amend the Employee Retirement Income Security Act, the Internal Revenue Code and the Public Health Service Act to require group health plans to provide a temporary continuation of group health coverage that otherwise might be terminated.

Benefits Disclosures and Notifications Checklist

- [ ] Children's Health Insurance Program (CHIP) Reauthorization Act Notice (if applicable to your state).
- [ ] FMLA General Notice (50 or more employees)
- [ ] HIPAA Notice of Privacy Practices (all plans).
- [ ] HIPAA Portability Special enrollment rights notice (all plans).
- [ ] Notice of Research Exception (for Genetic Information Non-Discrimination Act–GINA)
- [ ] Initial COBRA Notice (20+ employees) or State continuation notice (< 20 employees if required by your state).
- [ ] Medicare Part D Notice by October 15th (anyone eligible for Medicare).
- [ ] Mental Health Parity and Addiction Equity Notice (50 employees+).
- [ ] Newborn's and Mother's Health Protect Act Notice.
- [ ] Notice of Exchange for Employees (All employers to all employees) within 14 days of hire.
- [ ] Notice of Patient protections and Provider selections (all medical plans, if applicable).
- [ ] Provide participant's a list of ERISA rights (all ERISA plans).
- [ ] Qualified medical child support order receipt and determination handling—responds to such notices within 20 business days of the date of the notice.
- [ ] Register with the Center for Medicare Services regarding whether or not your prescription drug plan is creditable.
- [ ] Statement of Grandfathered status (only if you have a grandfathered plan).
- [ ] Summary of Material Modifications (SMM)—Given for modifications of the plan that are material within 210 days after the end of the plan year in which a modification or change is adopted. Communicates material plan reductions within 60 days of the change and plan terminations 60 days in advance.
- [ ] Uniform Summary of Benefits & Coverage (SBC)—Given to new participants upon application and annually to all participants for renewal.
- [ ] Wellness Program Disclosure (15 or more employees—ADA. If collecting health information)
- [ ] Wellness Programs Alternative Standards Notice (if offering a health-contingent wellness program in order to obtain a reward).
- [ ] Women's Health & Cancer Rights Act Notice (all plans).

Benefits Disclosures and Notifications Checklist

LEGAL CONCERNS

AFFORDABLE CARE ACT

The "Affordable Care Act" (ACA) is the name for the comprehensive health care reform law and its amendments. The law addresses health insurance coverage, health care costs, and preventive care. The law was enacted in two parts: The Patient Protection and Affordable Care Act was signed into law on March 23, 2010, and was amended by the Health Care and Education Reconciliation Act on March 30, 2010.

HIPAA

The Health Insurance Portability and Accountability Act of 1996 (HIPAA) is a federal law that requires the creation of national standards to protect sensitive patient health information from being disclosed without the patient's consent or knowledge.

COBRA

The Consolidated Omnibus Budget Reconciliation Act (COBRA) gives workers and their families who lose their health benefits the right to choose to continue group health benefits provided by their group health plan for limited periods under certain circumstances such as voluntary or involuntary job loss, reduction in the hours worked, the transition between jobs, death, divorce, and other life events. Qualified individuals may be required to pay the entire premium for coverage up to 102% of the cost to the plan.

FMLA

The Family and Medical Leave Act of 1993, as amended, (FMLA or Act) allows eligible employees of a covered employer to take job-protected, unpaid leave, or to substitute appropriate paid leave if the employee has earned or accrued it, for up to a total of 12 workweeks in any 12 months because of the birth of a child and to care for the newborn child, because of the placement of a child with the employee for adoption or foster care, because the employee is needed to care for a family member (child, spouse, or parent) with a severe health condition, because the employee's own serious health condition makes the employee unable to perform the functions of their job, or because of any qualifying exigency arising out of the fact that the employee's spouse, son, daughter, or parent is a military member on active duty or call to covered active duty status (or has been notified of an impending call or order to covered active duty).

Benefits Disclosures and Notifications Checklist

RESOURCES

Source: Code of Federal Regulations—Family Medical Leave Act
www.ecfr.gov/current/title-29/subtitle-B/chapter-V/subchapter-C/part-825

DOL.gov—Reporting and Disclosure Guide for Employee Benefit Plans
www.dol.gov/sites/dolgov/files/ebsa/about-ebsa/our-activities/resource-center/publications/reporting-and-disclosure-guide-for-employee-benefit-plans.pdf

Benefits Open Enrollment Checklist

PURPOSE

Open enrollment for benefits can be confusing as many things happen simultaneously. Taking an active approach and using this *Ultimate HR Checklist* can help you stay grounded and focused.

DEFINITIONS

Open Enrollment: Open enrollment is a period each year an employer will offer their employees a chance to sign up for health insurance or make changes to their plan. If an employee doesn't sign up during open enrollment, they will have to wait for the next open enrollment unless they are experiencing a qualifying event.

Qualifying Event: A qualifying event is a change in life circumstances that allows you to alter an existing health insurance policy or sign up for a new one outside of open enrollment periods. Without a qualifying event, you would need to wait until the next open enrollment period before making any changes. Common examples of qualifying events include the birth or adoption of a child, the death of a spouse, or a change in marital status.

Benefits Open Enrollment Checklist

- [ ] Review any areas of concern from the previous year regarding the process.
- [ ] Verify all employee addresses are correct.
- [ ] Develop a communication plan using various forms of media to notify and remind employees of upcoming benefits enrollment.
- [ ] Send out an official Open Enrollment notification announcement 30-45 days in advance.
  - Enrollment dates
  - Coverage effective dates
  - Reminder to update Beneficiaries
  - Proof of eligibility for new spouses or dependents
  - Preview of Plans and options
- [ ] Set up in-person or virtual info presentations for all employees at the beginning of Open Enrollment. Make them fun and informative.
- [ ] If possible, schedule the eligible employees to attend sessions.
- [ ] Continue to send reminders and notifications of key dates and actions.
- [ ] Be prepared to answer questions about legislative changes and any other healthcare concerns.
- [ ] Subject Matter Experts—Partner with your insurance broker or insurance representatives to attend and speak during the presentations.
- [ ] Provide employees with their current enrollment choices and payroll deductions.
- [ ] Ensure all eligible employees sign up for benefits or sign a waiver form declining benefits.
- [ ] Verify the new deduction amounts with employees before enrollment closes.
- [ ] Update your Payroll with the new deduction amounts.
- [ ] Send the data to your insurance carriers.
- [ ] Circle back with employees to confirm they received their ID cards.
- [ ] Analyze and compare current employee enrollments and participation with previous years to identify any trends in the plan changes.
- [ ] Keep any benefit enrollment and related medical paperwork in separate locked Benefit/Confidential files.

Benefits Open Enrollment Checklist

LEGAL CONCERNS

AFFORDABLE CARE ACT

The "Affordable Care Act" (ACA) is the name for the comprehensive health care reform law and its amendments. The law addresses health insurance coverage, health care costs, and preventive care. The law was enacted in two parts: The Patient Protection and Affordable Care Act was signed into law on March 23, 2010, and was amended by the Health Care and Education Reconciliation Act on March 30, 2010.

RESOURCES

What Is a Qualifying Event for Insurance? How It Works and Types
www.investopedia.com/terms/q/qualifying-event.asp

What to Do When You Miss Open Enrollment at Work
www.verywellhealth.com/what-is-open-enrollment-1738755

Leave Policy Checklist

PURPOSE

A solid employee-friendly Leave Policy can attract and retain employees. Some federal requirements for certain leaves and some states have additional requirements. Use this *Ultimate HR Checklist* to examine your current policy and ensure you cover all areas.

DEFINITIONS

Leave: Leave is a period granted by the employer to the employee to be excused from working.

Vacation Time: Vacation Time is leave granted to the employee to have a vacation away from work.

Sick Time: Sick Time is a leave granted to the employee because they or one of their immediate family members are ill. In some states and localities, paid sick time is required by law or regulation.

Personal Time Off (PTO): PTO is leave granted to an employee for whatever is necessary. Some organizations combine sick and vacation leave into one bucket called PTO.

Unlimited Time Off (UTO): UTO offers employees unlimited time off from their work.

Leave Policy Checklist

CREATING A LEAVE POLICY

- [ ] We offer the following types of leave
  - Sick
  - Personal Time Off (PTO)
  - Vacation Leave
  - Bereavement Leave
  - Holiday Leave
  - Voting Leave
  - State Domestic Violence Leave
  - Short Term Disability
  - Long Term Disability
  - FMLA Leave
  - State Paid Time off or FMLA
  - Parental Leave
  - Sabbatical Leave
  - Unpaid Leave
  - Jury Duty
  - Unlimited leave
- [ ] Review state and local laws to see what leave is regulated
- [ ] Decide who is entitled to each type of leave
  - By FLSA Status
  - By seniority
  - By level (Full Time and Part-Time)
  - Other (do not discriminate)
- [ ] Decide how much leave an individual employee will get each year
- [ ] Decide how often an employee can take time off and for how long
- [ ] Decide who is responsible for approving leave
- [ ] Decide on annual carryover
- [ ] Decide on when they need to notify you

Leave Policy Checklist

LEAVE POLICY IN ACTION

- [ ] Employee completed leave request form
- [ ] Manager or Supervisor reviews request
  - Is it an FMLA leave request?
  - Is it an ADA Accommodation Request?
- [ ] Manager approves, denies, or requests Human Resources Input
- [ ] Manager tracks leave based on company policy

LIST OF FEDERAL HOLIDAYS

- [ ] New Year's Day
- [ ] Birthday of Martin Luther King, Jr.
- [ ] Inauguration Day
- [ ] Washington's Birthday
- [ ] Memorial Day
- [ ] Juneteenth
- [ ] Independence Day
- [ ] Labor Day
- [ ] Columbus Day
- [ ] Veteran's Day
- [ ] Thanksgiving Day
- [ ] Christmas Day

Leave Policy Checklist

LEGAL CONCERNS

FMLA

The Family and Medical Leave Act of 1993, as amended, (FMLA or Act) allows eligible employees of a covered employer to take job-protected, unpaid leave, or to substitute appropriate paid leave if the employee has earned or accrued it, for up to a total of 12 workweeks in any 12 months because of the birth of a child and to care for the newborn child, because of the placement of a child with the employee for adoption or foster care, because the employee is needed to care for a family member (child, spouse, or parent) with a serious health condition, because the employee's own serious health condition makes the employee unable to perform the functions of their job, or because of any qualifying exigency arising out of the fact that the employee's spouse, son, daughter, or parent is a military member on active duty or call to covered active duty status (or has been notified of an impending call or order to covered active duty).

FAIR LABOR STANDARD ACT (FLSA)

Created in 1938, the Fair Labor Standard Acts sets the policies we use today to set proper compensation for our employees, including the federal minimum wage, the standard salary level, child labor laws, what is considered hours worked, correct record keeping, and the difference between those employees who receive overtime and those that do not.

FEDERAL AND STATE CONTRACTS

In some cases, your federal and state contracts may have vacation requirements built into them.

STATE AND LOCAL LAWS

Each state has its own set of regulations and laws regarding the type of leave employers need to grant their employees. Check with the agency that oversees your state's time off policies.

RESOURCES

US Department of Labor: Leave Benefits
www.dol.gov/general/topic/benefits-leave

Code of Federal Regulations
www.ecfr.gov/current/title-29/subtitle-A/part-4

Request for Time Off Form

PURPOSE

It is essential that when we offer employees time off, we create a system that allows us to be fair and consistent across the organization. Although not a checklist *per se*, it provides employers a systematic method to track their employee's time off.

DEFINITIONS

Leave: Leave is a period granted by the employer to the employee so they can be excused from working.

Vacation Time: Vacation Time is leave granted to the employee so that they can have a vacation away from work.

Sick Time: Sick Time is a leave granted to the employee because they or one of their immediate family members are ill. IN some states and localities, paid sick time is required by law or regulation.

Personal Time Off (PTO): PTO is leave granted to an employee for whatever the employee deems necessary. Some organizations combine sick, and vacation leave into one bucket called PTO.

Unlimited Time Off(UTO): UTO offers the employees unlimited time off from their work.

Request For Time Off Form

EMPLOYEE NAME: _____

EMPLOYEE ID#: _____

TODAY'S DATE: _____

TYPE OF LEAVE REQUEST

☐ Vacation	☐ Sick	☐ PTO
☐ Bereavement	☐ Holiday	☐ To Vote
☐ FMLA	☐ Sabbatical	☐ Parental Leave
☐ Jury Duty	☐ Unpaid Leave	☐ Other

START DATE: _____ END DATE: _____

Except for last-minute sick or personal time circumstances, all requests for leave must be submitted no later than one month before the start date of the request. The employee understands that all requests are subject to manager approval.

MANAGER APPROVAL

How many hours will the employee have in their leave bank? _____

How many hours will the employee use for this request? _____

☐ Accept   ☐ Deny

Reason for denying request: _____

_____

Manager's Signature: _____ Date: _____

If necessary, Human Resources signature: _____

Request for Time Off Form

LEGAL CONCERNS

FMLA

The Family and Medical Leave Act of 1993, as amended, (FMLA or Act) allows eligible employees of a covered employer to take job-protected, unpaid leave, or to substitute appropriate paid leave if the employee has earned or accrued it, for up to a total of 12 workweeks in any 12 months because of the birth of a child and to care for the newborn child, because of the placement of a child with the employee for adoption or foster care, because the employee is needed to care for a family member (child, spouse, or parent) with a serious health condition, because the employee's own serious health condition makes the employee unable to perform the functions of their job, or because of any qualifying exigency arising out of the fact that the employee's spouse, son, daughter, or parent is a military member on active duty or call to covered active duty status (or has been notified of an impending call or order to covered active duty).

FAIR LABOR STANDARD ACT (FLSA)

Created in 1938, the Fair Labor Standard Acts sets the policies we use today to set proper compensation for our employees, including the federal minimum wage, the standard salary level, child labor laws, what is considered hours worked, correct record keeping, and the difference between those employees who receive overtime and those that do not.

FEDERAL AND STATE CONTRACTS

In some cases, your federal and state contracts may have vacation requirements built into them.

State and Local Laws: Each state has its own set of regulations and laws regarding the type of leave employers need to grant their employees. Check with the agency that oversees your state's time off policies.

RESOURCES

US Department of Labor: Leave Benefits
www.dol.gov/general/topic/benefits-leave

Code of Federal Regulations
www.ecfr.gov/current/title-29/subtitle-A/part-4

Training Pay Checklist

PURPOSE

Under the FLSA, non-exempt employee's hours must be tracked and accounted for. According to Statue 29 C.F.R. 785.27, attendance at lectures, meetings, training programs, and similar activities need not be counted at working time if you can answer affirmatively to four questions.

DEFINITIONS

Training: Training is an obligation where an employee is required to attend.

Training Pay Checklist

- [ ] Is the training period or meeting held outside regular work hours?
- [ ] Is attendance fully voluntary?
- [ ] Is the training program or meeting not directly related to the employee's job? Does it teach them how to do their job better?
- [ ] Will the employee not perform any productive work while attending the course or meeting?

Training Pay Checklist

LEGAL CONCERNS

FAIR LABOR STANDARD ACT (FLSA)

Created in 1938, the Fair Labor Standard Acts sets the policies we use today to set proper compensation for our employees, including the federal minimum wage, the standard salary level, child labor laws, what is considered hours worked, correct record keeping, and the difference between those employees who receive overtime and those that do not.

RESOURCES

Travel Pay Checklist (page 152)

US Department of Labor: FLSA Hours Worked Advisor
webapps.dol.gov/elaws/whd/flsa/hoursworked/screenEr16.asp

US Department of Labor: Wage and Hours Fact Sheets
www.dol.gov/sites/dolgov/files/WHD/legacy/files/whdfs22.pdf

Travel Pay Checklist

PURPOSE

Under the FLSA, non-exempt employee's hours must be tracked and accounted for.

If you require your employees to travel, some of that time may be compensable. Travel should be compensated if the employee was "Suffered or Permitted" to work. Work not requested but suffered or permitted to be performed is work time that must be paid for by the employer. This *Ultimate HR Checklist* will help you determine those factors.

DEFINITIONS

Employ: By statutory definition, the term "employ" includes "to suffer or permit to work." The workweek ordinarily includes all time during which an employee is necessarily required to be on the employer's premises, on duty, or at a prescribed workplace.

"Workday," in general, means the period between the time on any particular day when such employee commences their "principal activity" and the time on that day at which they cease such principal activity or activities; therefore, the workday may be longer than the employee's scheduled shift, hours, tour of duty, or production line time.

Travel Time: The principles that determine whether time spent in travel is compensable time depend upon the kind of travel involved:

- *Home to Work Travel:* An employee who travels from home before the regular workday and returns to their home at the end of the workday is engaged in ordinary home to work travel, which does not count as work time.
- *Home to Work on a Special One Day Assignment in Another City:* An employee who regularly works at a fixed location in one city is given a special one-day assignment in another city and returns home the same day. The time spent traveling to and returning from the other city is work time, except that the employer may deduct/not count that time the employee would normally spend commuting to the regular work site.
- *Travel That is All in a Day's Work:* Time spent by an employee in travel as part of their principal activity, such as travel from job site to job site during the workday, is work time and must be counted as hours worked.
- *Travel Away from Home Community:* Travel that keeps an employee away from home overnight is travel away from home. Travel away from home is clearly work time when it cuts across the employee's workday. The time is not only hours worked on regular working days during normal working hours but also during corresponding hours on nonworking days. As an enforcement policy, the Division will not consider as work time that time spent in travel away from home outside of regular working hours as a passenger on an airplane, train, boat, bus, or automobile.

RESOURCES:

Fact Sheet #22
www.dol.gov/sites/dolgov/files/WHD/legacy/files/whdfs22.pdf

EMPLOYEES SHOULD BE COMPENSATED IF:

- [ ] Travel necessary to the work role and part of their principal activity. (Example: to go from job site to job site).
- [ ] The travel kept the employee away from home overnight.
- [ ] The travel occurred during "normal" work hours regardless of the workday, non-workday, or weekends.
- [ ] The employee worked while traveling. (prepared notes, answered emails, etc.).
- [ ] The trip takes place on a single day regardless of the regular business hours provision above. (Employee needs to go to a meeting in another town and returns on the same day.).
- [ ] Participation in an after-hours event that is mandatory.
- [ ] While on-call for situations if you cannot leave a building or hotel or are required to stay a certain distance away.

EMPLOYEES SHOULD NOT BE COMPENSATED IF:

- [ ] They travel on a plane, boat, bus, or vehicle as a passenger outside of regular work hours and do not perform any work-related duties.
- [ ] It is during rest or meal breaks when they are relieved of any work duties.
- [ ] Sleeping...unless on-call.
- [ ] The travel is considered a regular commute from home to work.
- [ ] They are attending a voluntary event, non-work-related lecture, meetings, or training outside of normal regular working hours.

Creating the Best Work Environment

ADA Interactive Process Checklist

PURPOSE

When an applicant or employee asks for a reasonable accommodation due to a disability, employers covered by the Americans with Disabilities Act (ADA) must consider it. The ADA Interactive Process *Ultimate HR Checklist* is a systematic approach to ensure companies properly consider any requests. While not directly required by law, following the ADA Interactive Steps can help a company stay safe and legal, show good faith, and document their consideration of the request.

DEFINITIONS

ADA: Americans with Disabilities Act. These initials will also cover the Americans with Disability Act Amendments Act.

Interactive Process: The Equal Employment Opportunity Commission (EEOC) recommends that all employers use the "interactive process" to make sure they are offering reasonable accommodations under the ADA.

Undue Hardship: Undue hardship means an accommodation would be a significant difficulty or expense to the employer based on several factors, including nature and cost of the accommodation, the size and resources of the company, and the employer's operational structure.

Direct Threat: The employer may require as part of the qualifications for the job that an individual will not be a "direct threat" to the health and safety of the individual and others. For instance, if putting an employee in a situation where there is a significant risk of substantial harm.

ADA Interactive Process Checklist

RECOGNIZE ACCOMMODATION REQUEST

- [ ] Conduct training for all supervisors in the ADA Process
- [ ] Fill out an accommodation request form
- [ ] Assign HR/Manager to guide the process

GATHER INFORMATION

- [ ] Confirm State and Federal ADA Requirements
- [ ] Review job description
- [ ] Talk to the manager about essential functions of the job
- [ ] Document conversation with the manager
- [ ] Meet with the employee to discuss limitations that impact their work
- [ ] Document conversation with the employee
- [ ] If appropriate, request medical documentation
- [ ] Use www.askJAN.org to gather additional information
- [ ] Identify employee's limitation

EXPLORING ACCOMMODATION

- [ ] Keep an open mind
- [ ] Brainstorm possible accommodations using employee's input
- [ ] If applicable, ask the employee's medical provider for ideas
- [ ] Document conversation with the medical provider and the employee
- [ ] Refer to www.askJAN.org for ideas
- [ ] Review accommodations for undue hardship to the company
- [ ] Review accommodations for direct threat protection

ADA Interactive Process Checklist

CHOOSE ACCOMMODATION
- [ ] Consider the employee's preference
- [ ] Decide on accommodation and note the reason
- [ ] Decide on the length of a trial period
- [ ] Communicate to manager and employee the accommodation
- [ ] Protect confidentiality
- [ ] Document conversations

IMPLEMENT ACCOMMODATION
- [ ] Assign a manager to oversee the implementation of the selected accommodation
- [ ] Create project timeline and communicate to impacted individuals
- [ ] Track costs
- [ ] Allow the employee to test the accommodation before signing off

MONITORING THE ACCOMMODATION
- [ ] Assign a manager to oversee the accommodation
- [ ] Regularly check on the effectiveness of the accommodation
- [ ] If applicable, maintain the accommodation
- [ ] Encourage on-going conversations
- [ ] Update accommodation as necessary based on changing environment

MANAGERS AND SUPERVISORS ADA TRAINING CHECKLIST
- [ ] ADAAA Title I and Title V
- [ ] Discrimination
- [ ] Definition of Disability
- [ ] Pre-hiring Restrictions
- [ ] Post-offer Testing
- [ ] Reasonable Accommodations
- [ ] Interactive Process
- [ ] Undue Hardship
- [ ] Direct Threat

ADA Interactive Process Checklist

LEGAL CONCERNS

AMERICANS WITH DISABILITIES ACT

The ADA requires employers with fifteen or more employees to provide effective accommodations for covered employees with disability.

AMERICANS WITH DISABILITIES ACT AMENDMENTS ACT

The ADAAA further clarifies who has a disability and what the employer must do.

STATE AND LOCAL DISABILITY LAWS

In some instances, the state and local governments may have other disability laws that must be followed. In the resources section below, we provide a link.

RESOURCES

The Americans with Disabilities Act (ADA) protects people with disabilities from discrimination.
www.ada.gov

Job Accommodations Network
www.askjan.org
askjan.org/topics/interactive.cfm
askjan.org/publications/ada-specific/Technical-Assistance-Manual-for-Title-I-of-the-ADA.cfm

State Regulations
www.law.cornell.edu/regulations

ADA Interactive Questions Checklists

PURPOSE

The ADA Interactive process is used to help an employer understand the appropriate accommodation to offer an employee with a disability. The following questions help guide the HR practitioner in understanding the employee's situation better, defining the limitations, and offering an accommodation. These Questions Aim to foster a collaborative and supportive approach to ADA compliance, ensuring that individuals with disabilities are provided with the accommodation and support they need to thrive.

DEFINITIONS:

ADA: Americans with Disabilities Act. These initials will also cover the Americans with Disability Act Amendments Act.

Interactive Process: The Equal Employment Opportunity Commission (EEOC) recommends that all employers use the "interactive process" to make sure they are offering reasonable accommodations under the ADA.

Undue Hardship: Undue hardship means an accommodation would be a significant difficulty or expense to the employer based on several factors, including the nature and cost of the accommodation, the size and resources of the company, and the employer's operational structure.

Direct Threat: The employer may require that as part of the qualifications for the job, an individual will not be a "direct threat" to the health and safety of the individual and others. For instance, if putting an employee in a situation with a significant risk of substantial harm.

ADA Interactive Questions Checklist

UNDERSTANDING THE DISABILITY

1. Understanding the Disability:
   - Can you describe how your disability impacts your ability to perform essential job functions or participate in activities?
   - What accommodations have you used in the past that have been effective?
   - Are there any specific tasks or environments that present challenges for you due to your disability?

2. Job-related Questions:
   - Can you describe your typical workday and the tasks you perform?
   - Are there any aspects of your job that you find particularly challenging due to your disability?
   - What support or resources do you believe would enhance your performance and job satisfaction?
   - Accommodation Needs:
   - What accommodations do you believe would enable you to perform your job duties effectively?
   - Have you consulted with any healthcare professionals or specialists regarding potential accommodations?
   - Are there any temporary accommodations that could be implemented while we explore longer-term solutions?

3. Communication and Collaboration:
   - How can we ensure effective communication and collaboration between you, your supervisor, HR, and any other relevant stakeholders?
   - Are there specific communication preferences or assistive technologies that would facilitate your participation in meetings or discussions?
   - What strategies can we implement to promote a supportive and inclusive work environment for all employees?

4. Future Planning:
   - Are there any potential changes or accommodations that may be needed as your job responsibilities evolve?
   - How can we proactively address any new challenges or barriers that may arise in the future?
   - Would you be open to periodic check-ins to assess the effectiveness of accommodations and make any necessary adjustments?

5. Confidentiality and Privacy:
   - How would you prefer information about your disability and accommodations to be handled in terms of confidentiality and privacy?
   - Are there any concerns you have regarding potential stigma or discrimination related to your disability?

ADA Interactive Questions Checklist

6. Resources and Support:
   - Are you aware of any resources or support services available through the company or external organizations that could benefit you?
   - How can we ensure that you have access to the necessary training and support to succeed in your role?

7. Interactive Process Feedback:
   - How do you feel about the interactive process so far? Is there anything you would like to see done differently?
   - Do you have any concerns or questions about the ADA and its application to your situation?
   - Are there any barriers to accessing accommodations or participating fully in the interactive process?

ADA Interactive Questions Checklist

LEGAL CONCERNS

AMERICANS WITH DISABILITIES ACT

The ADA requires employers with fifteen or more employees to provide effective accommodations for covered employees with disability.

AMERICANS WITH DISABILITIES ACT AMENDMENTS ACT

The ADAAA further clarifies who has a disability and what the employer must do.

STATE AND LOCAL DISABILITY LAWS

In some instances, the state and local governments may have other disability laws that must be followed. In the resources section below, we provide a link

RESOURCES

U.S. Department of Justice—Civil Rights Division
www.ada.gov/

Job Accommodation Network
www.askjan.org
askjan.org/topics/interactive.cfm
askjan.org/publications/ada-specific/Technical-Assistance-Manual-for-Title-I-of-the-ADA.cfm

State Regulations
www.law.cornell.edu/regulations

Accommodation Request Form

This form is to be completed when an employee or candidate is requesting an accommodation to do their job's essential functions as described in the job description.

Company: _____

Name: _____

Employee ID: _____ Date _____

Position: _____ Department: _____

Manager: _____

HR: _____

1. Accommodation Requested:

2. Medical Provider Notes:

3. Possible Accommodations:

4. Chosen Accommodation:

5. Implementation Plan:

Anti-Harassment & Anti-Discrimination Policy Checklist

PURPOSE

Employers need to protect their employees from harassment and discrimination. The first line of defense is a clear and concise anti-harassment and discrimination policy based on the Civil Rights Act of 1964—Title VII and the Equal Employment Opportunity Commission (EEOC). In fact, the EEOC says that employers must "provide reasonable care" to their employees. A policy, training, and enforcing it are essential steps to keeping employers legal and safe by showing a good-faith effort.

DEFINITIONS

Title VII of the Civil Rights Act of 1964: Title VII prohibits employment discrimination based on race, color, religion, sex, and national origin. All employers in the United States with fifteen or more employees for each working day in each of twenty or more calendar weeks in the current or preceding calendar year.

Anti-Harassment And Anti-Discrimination Policy Checklist

☐ State that discrimination based on race, color, religion, sex (including pregnancy, sexual orientation, or gender identity), national origin, disability, age (40 or older), or genetic information (including family medical history) is illegal and will not be tolerated. Provide definitions and good examples of prohibited conduct, as needed.

☐ State that you will provide reasonable accommodations (changes to the way things are generally done at work) to applicants and employees who need them for medical or religious reasons, as required by law.

☐ Explain how employees can report discrimination.

- If possible, designate more than one person to receive and respond to discrimination complaints or questions.
- Consider permitting employees to report the discrimination to any manager.

☐ State that employees will not be punished for reporting discrimination, participating in a discrimination investigation or lawsuit, or opposing discrimination.

☐ State that you protect the confidentiality of employees who report discrimination or participate in a discrimination investigation to the greatest possible extent.

☐ Require managers and other employees with human resources responsibilities to respond appropriately to discrimination or report it to individuals who are authorized to respond.

☐ Provide for a prompt, thorough, and impartial investigation of complaints.

☐ Provide prompt and effective corrective and preventative action when necessary.

☐ Consider requiring that employees who file internal complaints be notified about the status of their complaint, the investigation results, and any corrective and preventative action taken.

☐ Describe the consequences of violating the non-discrimination policy.

- Federal, state, and local laws may prohibit additional types of discrimination and/or require you to provide reasonable accommodations for other reasons. Federal, state, and local government websites may have additional information about these laws.

Anti-Harassment And Anti-Discrimination Policy Checklist

LEGAL CONCERNS

TITLE VII OF THE CIVIL RIGHTS ACT OF 1964

Title VII prohibits employment discrimination based on race, color, religion, sex, and national origin. All employers in the United States with fifteen or more employees for each working day in each of twenty or more calendar weeks in the current or preceding calendar year.

DISCRIMINATION CAN HAPPEN NUMEROUS TIMES OF THE EMPLOYEE LIFE CYCLE, INCLUDING:

- job advertisements and postings
- employment references, job referrals
- discipline and discharge
- application and hiring practices
- job assignments and promotions
- reasonable accommodations and disability
- pay and benefits
- recruitment practices
- training and apprenticeship programs

    Employers must be careful not to unintentionally or intentionally discriminate against their employees and candidates applying for jobs.

DISCRIMINATION LAWS INCLUDE BUT ARE NOT LIMITED TO:

- Pregnant Workers Fairness Act
- Civil Rights Act of 1964–Title VII
- Americans with Disabilities Act
- Age Discrimination in Employment Act
- Pregnancy Act of 1978
- Equal Pay Act of 1963
- Genetic Information Non-discrimination Act (GINA)
- Vietnam Era Veteran's Readjustment Act (VEVRA)

    NOTE: Do not forget to familiarize yourself with state and local employment laws.

Anti-Harassment And Anti-Discrimination Policy Checklist

RESOURCES

U.S. Equal Employment Opportunity Commission
www.eeoc.gov
www.eeoc.gov/employers
www.eeoc.gov/employers/small-business/general-non-discrimination-policy-tips

State Regulations
www.law.cornell.edu/regulations

Sourced from EEOC Guidelines

Family Medical Leave Act Checklist

PURPOSE

The federal Family and Medical Leave Act (FMLA) is designed to help employees balance their work and family responsibilities by allowing them to take reasonable unpaid leave for specific family and medical reasons. It also seeks to accommodate the legitimate interests of employers and promote equal employment opportunities for men and women.

FMLA provides certain employees with 12 weeks of unpaid, job-protected leave per 12 months. It also requires that their group health benefits be maintained during the leave, and some states have additional protections. The *Ultimate HR Checklist* below is based on federal guidelines and law.

DEFINITIONS

Employer: Any person engaged in commerce or an industry or activity affecting business that employs 50 or more employees for each working day during each of 20 or more calendar workweeks in the current or preceding calendar year.

Employee: Any individual employed by an employer.

Key employee: A salaried FMLA-eligible employee who is among the highest-paid 10 percent of all the employees employed by the employer within 75 miles of the employee's worksite.

Hours of Service: The FMLA uses the FLSA principles for determining compensable hours and generally does not include benefit time, i.e., vacation, sick time, personal time off, etc.

Family Medical Leave Act Checklist

DOES YOUR ORGANIZATION FALL UNDER THE FAMILY MEDICAL LEAVE ACT? (ONLY ONE NEED APPLY)

- ☐ Private-sector employer, with 50 or more employees in 20 or more workweeks in the current or preceding calendar year, including a joint employer or successor in interest to a covered employer;
- ☐ Public agency, including a local, state, or Federal government agency, regardless of the number of employees it employs; or
- ☐ Public or private elementary or secondary school, regardless of the number of employees it employs.

DOES YOUR EMPLOYEE FALL UNDER THE FAMILY MEDICAL LEAVE ACT? (ALL MUST APPLY)

- ☐ Works for a *covered employer*;
- ☐ Has worked for the employer for at least 12 months;
- ☐ Has at least *1,250 hours of service* for the employer during the 12 months immediately preceding the leave; and
- ☐ Works at a location where the employer has at least *50 employees within 75 miles.*
- ☐ Hang Poster Up.
- ☐ Decide if you will use a calendar year or rolling calendar for the FMLA 12 month period.
- ☐ Add FMLA Policy to your employee handbook.
- ☐ Train Supervisors and Managers to recognize an FMLA Request.
- ☐ Upon acquiring knowledge that leave may be for an FMLA-qualifying reason, provide the employee with notice concerning their eligibility for FMLA leave.
- ☐ Must be one or more of the following reasons:
  - The birth of a son or daughter or placement of a son or daughter with the employee for adoption or foster care;
  - To care for a spouse, son, daughter, or parent who has a serious health condition;
  - For a serious health condition that makes the employee unable to perform the essential functions of their job; or
  - For any qualifying exigency arising out of the fact that a spouse, son, daughter, or parent is a military member on covered active duty or call to covered active-duty status.
- ☐ Complete Form WH-381 within five days of notification.

Family Medical Leave Act Checklist

- [ ] Inform the employee of their rights and responsibilities under FMLA.
    - Restoration of their job
    - The use of unpaid leave
    - Ability to maintain health benefits
    - Ability to maintain other benefits such as life insurance and pensions
    - Requirements to furnish periodic progress reports while out
- [ ] If appropriate—request the employee to have the healthcare provider complete the relevant certification forms. (Must be returned in 15 days).
- [ ] If appropriate—request employee to complete for FMLA military leave (Must be returned in 15 days).
- [ ] Complete WH-382.
- [ ] If necessary, request and pay for 2nd and 3rd opinions.
- [ ] Discuss with employee return to work requirements.
- [ ] Track the hour's employee does not work based on FMLA.
- [ ] Request Progress Reports.
- [ ] Request and review Return to Work Documentation.
- [ ] Welcome employee back.

NOTE: Do not forget to review your state and local leave laws.

Family Medical Leave Act Checklist

LEGAL CONCERNS

FMLA

The Family and Medical Leave Act of 1993, as amended, (FMLA or Act) allows eligible employees of a covered employer to take job-protected, unpaid leave, or to substitute appropriate paid leave if the employee has earned or accrued it, for up to a total of 12 workweeks in any 12 months because of the birth of a child and to care for the newborn child, because of the placement of a child with the employee for adoption or foster care, because the employee is needed to care for a family member (child, spouse, or parent) with a serious health condition, because the employee's own serious health condition makes the employee unable to perform the functions of their job, or because of any qualifying exigency arising out of the fact that the employee's spouse, son, daughter, or parent is a military member on active duty or call to covered active duty status (or has been notified of an impending call or order to covered active duty).

Source: www.ecfr.gov/current/title-29/subtitle-B/chapter-V/subchapter-C/part-825

It is unlawful for any employer to interfere with, restrain, or deny the exercise of or the attempt to exercise any right provided by the FMLA. It is also unlawful for an employer to discharge or discriminate against any individual for opposing any practice or because of involvement in any proceeding related to the FMLA.

See Fact Sheet 77B (www.dol.gov/agencies/whd/fact-sheets/77b-fmla-protections): Protections for Individuals under the FMLA. The Wage and Hour Division is responsible for administering and enforcing the FMLA for most employees. Most federal and certain congressional employees are also covered by the law but are subject to the jurisdiction of the U.S. Office of Personnel Management or Congress.

Source: www.dol.gov/agencies/whd/fact-sheets/28-fmla

RESOURCES

Family and Medical Leave (FMLA)
www.dol.gov/general/topic/benefits-leave/fmla

Wage and Hour Division Fact Sheets
www.dol.gov/sites/dolgov/files/WHD/legacy/files/whdfs28.pdf

The Family and Medical Leave Act of 1993
www.ecfr.gov/current/title-29/subtitle-B/chapter-V/subchapter-C/part-825

Race and Color Discrimination Prevention Checklist

PURPOSE

Preventing all discrimination in the workplace should be your goal. Some discriminatory behaviors are apparent and, when noticed, can be corrected. Other discriminatory behaviors maybe not be so apparent and harder to recognize. This can lead to something called "disparate impact." When it comes to race and color discrimination, disparate impact is more prevalent. This *Ultimate HR Checklist* will help you avoid disparate impact discrimination, specifically with race and color.

DEFINITIONS

Disparate Treatment: Under Title VII of the Civil Rights Act, Disparate Treatment is when an employer treats an applicant or employee differently because of their membership in a protected class. The issue is whether the employer's actions were motivated by discriminatory intent. Discriminatory intent can either be shown by direct evidence or through indirect or circumstantial evidence.

Disparate Impact: Under Title VII of the Civil Rights Act of 1964, Disparate Impact is unintentional discrimination when an organization's policies, practices, and procedures appear to be neutral but result in a disproportionate impact on a protected group.

EEO: Equal Employment Opportunity. Under Title VII of the Civil Rights Act, employers must provide equal opportunity (treat fairly) to both applicants and employees. Employers cannot use specific characteristics such as race and national origin to make employment decisions.

Race and Color Discrimination Prevention Checklist

HOW CAN YOUR COMPANY PREVENT RACE AND COLOR DISCRIMINATION IN THE WORKPLACE?

- [ ] Train Human Resources managers and all employees on EEO laws.
- [ ] Implement a firm EEO policy that is embraced at the top levels of the organization.
- [ ] Train managers, supervisors, and employees on your policy enforce it and hold them accountable.
- [ ] Foster open communication and early dispute resolution.
- [ ] Establish neutral and objective criteria to avoid subjective employment decisions based on personal stereotypes or hidden biases.

RECRUITMENT, HIRING, AND PROMOTION

- [ ] Recruit, hire and promote with EEO principles in mind by implementing practices designed to widen and diversify the pool of candidates.
- [ ] Conduct self-audits to determine whether current employment practices disadvantage people of color or treat them differently.
- [ ] Ensure selection criteria do not disproportionately exclude certain racial groups unless the standards are valid predictors of successful job performance and meet your business needs.
- [ ] Make sure promotion criteria are made known and that job openings are communicated to all eligible employees.
- [ ] When using an outside agency for recruitment, make sure the agency does not search for candidates of a particular race or color.

TERMS, CONDITIONS, AND PRIVILEGES OF EMPLOYMENT

- [ ] Monitor compensation practices and performance appraisal systems for patterns of potential discrimination.
- [ ] Performance appraisals are based on employees' actual job performance.
- [ ] Ensure consistency, i.e., that comparable job performances receive comparable ratings regardless of the evaluator and that appraisals are neither artificially low nor artificially high.
- [ ] Develop the potential of employees, supervisors, and managers with EEO in mind, by providing training and mentoring.
- [ ] Provide transparent and credible assurances that if employees make complaints or provide information related to complaints, you will protect them from retaliation.

Race and Color Discrimination Prevention Checklist

LEGAL CONCERNS

TITLE VII OF THE CIVIL RIGHTS ACT OF 1964

This law makes it illegal to discriminate against someone based on race, color, religion, national origin, or sex. The law also makes it unlawful to retaliate against a person because they complained about discrimination, filed a charge of discrimination, or participated in an employment discrimination investigation or lawsuit. The law also requires that employers reasonably accommodate applicants' and employees' sincerely held religious practices unless doing so would impose an undue hardship on the operation of the employer's business or other national laws set standards of discrimination such as the Pregnancy Act of 1978, Age Discrimination in Employment Act, etc.

RESOURCES

Electronic Code of Federal Regulations: Title 29—Labor: Disparate Treatment
www.law.cornell.edu/cfr/text/29/1607.11

5 Powerful Ways to Take REAL Action on DEI (Diversity, Equity & Inclusion)
www.ccl.org/articles/leading-effectively-articles/5-powerful-ways-to-take-real-action-on-dei-diversity-equity-inclusion

15 Key Benefits Of DEI To Communicate With Team Members
www.forbes.com/sites/forbeshumanresourcescouncil/2021/05/19/15-key-benefits-of-dei-to-communicate-with-team-members

Investigating a Harassment Complaint

PURPOSE

All harassment complaints should be investigated. The Supreme Court has ruled that employers could have an "affirmative defense" if the employer exercised reasonable care to prevent and promptly correct any sexually harassing behavior. Having a prompt and thorough investigation process is a practice that the EEOC and courts consider to be a best practice. This workplace harassment complaint investigation *Ultimate HR Checklist* guides employers and human resource professionals through investigative steps to help protect the organization.

DEFINITIONS

Harassment: Harassment is a form of employment discrimination that violates Title VII of the Civil Rights Act of 1964, the Age Discrimination in Employment Act of 1967 (ADEA), and the Americans with Disabilities Act of 1990 (ADA). Harassment is unwelcome conduct that is based on race, color, religion, sex (including sexual orientation, gender identity, or pregnancy), national origin, older age (beginning at age 40), disability, or genetic information (including family medical history). Harassment becomes unlawful where 1) enduring the offensive conduct becomes a condition of continued employment, or 2) the conduct is severe or pervasive enough to create a work environment that a reasonable person would consider intimidating, hostile, or abusive. Anti-discrimination laws also prohibit harassment against individuals in retaliation for filing a discrimination charge, testifying, or participating in any way in an investigation, proceeding, or lawsuit under these laws; or opposing employment practices that they reasonably believe discriminate against individuals, in violation of these laws.–www.eeoc.gov/harassment

Witness: In the case of harassment, the investigation is important that an additional person (witness) is present when interviews take place. The witness should remain quiet, take notes, and if necessary be a neutral representative.

Investigating a Harassment Complaint

EXAMPLE POLICY: ANTI-HARASSMENT AND DISCRIMINATION

Our organization believes in the power of diversity and inclusivity and welcomes everyone. Discrimination based on race, color, religion, sex (including pregnancy, sexual orientation, gender identity), national origin, disability, and age (40 and older) or genetic information (including family medical history) is illegal and will not be tolerated within our organization. When necessary, we will provide reasonable accommodations to applicants and employees who need them for medical or religious reasons as required by law.

Any violation of this policy should be reported directly to your supervisor, any organizational leader, or designated human resources contact. Complaints will be promptly and thoroughly investigated. When our policy is violated, it could lead to the termination of the accused harasser.

Our company has a firm no retaliation policy. Any individual who retaliates against a person reporting a complaint to our organization will be immediately terminated. We will do our best to protect the complainant's confidentiality to the greatest extent possible.

Investigating a Harassment Complaint

- [ ] Receive the complaint
    - Each company must have a defined process to receive harassment complaints by employees
- [ ] Review company's anti-harassment policy
- [ ] Start the investigation immediately!
- [ ] Review complaint with the complainant
    - Review anti-harassment and discrimination policy
    - Preserve confidentiality but do not promise it
    - Ask questions to fully understand complaint—Who, What, Where, and When
    - Discuss expected outcome
    - Ask for any witnesses, either internal or external
    - Ask for any additional documentation
    - Obtain background information about the complainant
    - Have them write out the complaint and sign it
- [ ] Make sure the complainant is safe and free from further harassment during the investigation
- [ ] If necessary, remove the alleged harasser from the same work vicinity as the complainant for the duration of the investigation
- [ ] Determine the focus and goal of the investigation
- [ ] Determine who is involved
    - Complainant(s)
    - Alleged harasser
    - Co-workers and other witnesses
    - External witnesses
- [ ] Appoint an unbiased investigator
- [ ] Appoint an unbiased witness and dedicated note-taker
- [ ] Develop an investigation plan
- [ ] Prepare to interview people involved
- [ ] Schedule interviews—move quickly
- [ ] Review personnel files and prior relevant complaints
- [ ] Review Employee Handbook and impacted policies

Investigating a Harassment Complaint

- [ ] Interview the alleged harasser
  - Introduce yourself, witness, and the nature of the complaint
  - Review anti-harassment and discrimination policy
  - Preserve confidentiality but do not promise it
  - Remind them of the no retaliation policy
  - Obtain background information about the alleged harasser
  - Ask open-ended questions to investigate the complaint
  - Ask for additional documentation or witnesses
  - Let them know the process
- [ ] Interview other selected personnel
  - Have a witness
  - Discuss the importance of confidentiality
  - Explain the purpose of the interview in general terms
  - Obtain background information
  - Ask questions to investigate the complaint
  - Ask about additional documentation or witnesses
  - Explain that upon completion, the company will attempt to determine what occurred and will take appropriate action
  - Remind each interviewee that retaliation in any form is forbidden and could lead to termination. The employer should have zero tolerance for retaliation
  - Ask each witness to prepare their written documents about what occurred.
  - Ask open-ended questions
- [ ] Document the interview (decide if you want to record them)
- [ ] Use forms to capture stated information and reactions of people being interviewed
- [ ] Review any other pertinent data—videotapes, emails, recorded conversations, etc.
- [ ] Explore previous discipline action of the interviewees
- [ ] Explore the relationship between the complainant and the alleged harasser
- [ ] Discuss with the investigation team
- [ ] Analyze the findings
  - Summarize the interviews
  - Create a timeline of events
  - Summarize the documentations
  - Establish and identify the credibility of all involved
  - Identify any inaccuracies—go back and follow up
  - Consult with an attorney before ruling

Investigating a Harassment Complaint

- [ ] Conclude what happened
- [ ] Determine next action steps based on defined policies
- [ ] Take action
  - Request an apology
  - Issue a discipline notice
  - Change job assignment of the harasser
  - Remove bonus
  - Suspend without pay
  - Terminate
- [ ] Create a report
- [ ] If unlawful activities took place, immediately let authorities know
- [ ] Keep documentation outside of personnel file
- [ ] Communicate to the alleged harasser, complainant, and the executive team

Investigating a Harassment Complaint

LEGAL CONCERNS

HARASSMENT

The EEOC defines harassment as unwelcome conduct that is based on race, color, religion, sex (including pregnancy), national origin, age (40 or older), disability, or genetic information. Harassment becomes unlawful where 1) enduring the offensive conduct becomes a condition of continued employment, or 2) the conduct is severe or pervasive enough to create a work environment that a reasonable person would consider intimidating, hostile, or abusive.

RESOURCES

U.S. Equal Employment Opportunity Commission—Harassment
www.eeoc.gov/harassment

U.S. Equal Employment Opportunity Commission—Youth Harassment
www.eeoc.gov/youth/harassment

Harassment Reporting Form

PURPOSE

Taking prompt, thorough action when a complaint of harassment occurs could save organizations a lawsuit and prompt positive employee relations. It states that harassing behaviors of any kind will not be tolerated in the workplace. Often, managers in the field receive complaints but are unsure how to handle them. This *Ultimate HR Checklist* is in a form format to provide to employees who make complaints. It is the first step that should be taken and then immediately forwarded to Human Resources or senior leadership.

DEFINITIONS

Harassment: Harassment is a form of employment discrimination that violates Title VII of the Civil Rights Act of 1964, the Age Discrimination in Employment Act of 1967 (ADEA), and the Americans with Disabilities Act of 1990 (ADA). Harassment is unwelcome conduct that is based on race, color, religion, sex (including sexual orientation, gender identity, or pregnancy), national origin, older age (beginning at age 40), disability, or genetic information (including family medical history). Harassment becomes unlawful where 1) enduring the offensive conduct becomes a condition of continued employment, or 2) the conduct is severe or pervasive enough to create a work environment that a reasonable person would consider intimidating, hostile, or abusive. Anti-discrimination laws also prohibit harassment against individuals in retaliation for filing a discrimination charge, testifying, or participating in any way in an investigation, proceeding, or lawsuit under these laws; or opposing employment practices that they reasonably believe discriminate against individuals, in violation of these laws.

—www.eeoc.gov/harassment

Harassment Reporting Form

Please complete this form if you are experiencing harassment in our company. Harassment of any kind goes against our set of employee values and will not be tolerated. Every complaint will be thoroughly investigated by an independent investigator as assigned by human resources.

Name of the person reporting the complaint: _____

Department: _____

Phone Number: _____ Email: _____

Name of Accused Person(s): _____

Title of Accused Person if known: _____

Department of Accused Person: _____

Phone Number of Accused Person: _____

What is the basis for your complaint?

- ☐ Abusive Conduct
- ☐ Discrimination
- ☐ Harassment
- ☐ Workplace Violence
- ☐ Inappropriate Comments
- ☐ Inappropriate Behaviors
- ☐ Retaliation

In your own words, explain what happened; please include the following:

- Time Frame—how often it happened
- Who was involved?
- If any, who witnessed the events?
- Where did it happen, be as specific as possible?
- What happened?

Harassment Reporting Form

Were other workers treated similarly? ☐ Yes ☐ No

If yes, please provide a list of names below.

Please provide the names of any additional people who could give supporting information.

- Witnesses
- Coworkers
- Supervisors
- Managers
- Customers/Clients

Please identify any information that may be relevant to this matter.

- Diaries/Journals
- Calendars
- Recordings
- Emails
- Voicemails
- Texts
- Social Media Posts
- Correspondence

What do you want to happen as a result of this complaint?

Signature of Complainant: _____

Date: _____

_____

Date Received: _____ By Whom: _____

Assigned to: _____ Date Assigned: _____

Harassment Reporting Form

LEGAL CONCERNS

TITLE VII OF THE CIVIL RIGHTS ACT OF 1964

Title VII prohibits employment discrimination based on race, color, religion, sex, and national origin. All employers in the United States with fifteen or more employees for each working day in each of twenty or more calendar weeks in the current or preceding calendar year. Harassment is considered discrimination.

RESOURCES

U.S. Equal Employment Opportunity Commission—Harassment
www.eeoc.gov/harassment

U.S. Equal Employment Opportunity Commission—Youth Harassment
www.eeoc.gov/youth/harassment

Workplace Investigations Checklist

PURPOSE

There are many reasons to conduct workplace investigations. Each employee complaint and subsequent workplace investigation is unique and different. It is important to have a consistent process for efficiency, consistency, and protection against lawsuits. There are numerous types of investigations, including discriminatory practices, harassment, bullying, workplace theft, or confidentiality agreements. The *Ultimate HR Checklist* below will help give a structure to your investigation process no matter the reason.

DEFINITIONS

Workplace: A workplace is where an individual or group of employees perform tasks and responsibilities on behalf of an employer. These can be at the owner's worksite or at the individual employee's home or remote office.

Workplace Investigations Checklist

DEFINE THE SCOPE OF THE INVESTIGATION—HAVE A PLAN

- [ ] Who is being investigated?
- [ ] Why are they being investigated?
- [ ] Who will be interviewed?
- [ ] Are there any written witness statements?
- [ ] Is there any video footage or other records to consider (time cards, access logs, etc.)
- [ ] Gather any physical evidence (email messages, text messages, written notes, etc.)

NOTIFYING EMPLOYEE UNDER INVESTIGATION

- [ ] Advise employee complaint has been made in private
- [ ] Advise the employee of particulars of complaint (i.e., who, what, where, when)
- [ ] Afford employee opportunity to respond to each allegation
- [ ] Remind the employee being investigated of retaliation and reprisal actions
- [ ] Discuss confidentiality expectations during the investigation

TRAITS TO CONSIDER WHEN SELECTING AN INVESTIGATOR

- [ ] Neutral, unbiased, and impartial
- [ ] Patient, calm, approachable
- [ ] Tech savvy for remote investigations

INVESTIGATION INTERVIEW DYNAMICS

- [ ] Lay out ground rules
- [ ] Use open-ended questions to draw out more information
- [ ] Avoid aggressive techniques—be professional and courteous
- [ ] Remind all employees again about retaliation and reprisal
- [ ] Document everything—consider a third party to document the interview
- [ ] Never share details with colleagues that are not involved in the situation

Workplace Investigations Checklist

WRAP UP

- [ ] Create a final report with a conclusion and action taken
- [ ] Submit finding to the decision-maker
- [ ] Inform employee who made the complaint that action was taken
- [ ] Document your follow-up with any activities that arise out of the investigation, including discipline taken and new policies/procedures created
- [ ] Determine if training is needed to prevent a similar situation in the future
- [ ] Specifically, remind managers and other leaders that retaliation in any form is unacceptable, puts the organization at risk, and is grounds for immediate termination

Workplace Investigations Checklist

LEGAL CONCERNS

TITLE VII OF THE CIVIL RIGHTS ACT OF 1964

Title VII prohibits employment discrimination based on race, color, religion, sex, and national origin. All employers in the United States with fifteen or more employees for each working day in each of twenty or more calendar weeks in the current or preceding calendar year. Harassment is considered discrimination.

OCCUPATIONAL SAFETY AND HEALTH

According to the general clause of OSHA, employers are required to have a workplace free from recognized hazards that may cause death or serious harm. It is unethical to disregard or blatantly ignore the safety of our team members.

FAIR LABOR STANDARD ACT (FLSA)

Created in 1938, the Fair Labor Standard Acts sets the policies we use today to set proper compensation for our employees, including the federal minimum wage, the standard salary level, child labor laws, what is considered hours worked, correct record keeping, and the difference between those employees who receive overtime and those that do not.

RESOURCES

U.S. Equal Employment Opportunity Commission
www.eeoc.gov

Six Types of Investigations Coming Soon to a Workplace Near You
www.wagenerlaw.com/articles/Six_Types_of_Investigations_Coming_Soon_to_a_Workplace_Near_You

The Pregnant Workers Fairness Act Checklist

PURPOSE

The Pregnant Workers Fairness Act (PWFA) is a new law that goes into effect on June 27, 2023 and requires covered employers to provide "reasonable accommodations" to a worker's known limitations related to pregnancy, childbirth, or related medical conditions, unless the accommodation will cause the employer an "undue hardship."

DEFINITIONS

ADA: The Americans with Disability Act protects people with disabilities from discrimination. Disability rights are civil rights. From voting to parking, the ADA is a law that protects people with disabilities in many areas of public life.

Reasonable Accommodation: Any change to the application or hiring process, to the job, to the way the job is done, or the work environment that allows a person with a disability who is qualified for the job to perform the essential functions of that job and enjoy equal employment opportunities. Accommodations are considered "reasonable" if they do not create an undue hardship or a direct threat.

The Pregnant Workers Fairness Act Checklist

COVERED EMPLOYEES

- [ ] Employers with 15 or more employees, including:
  - Private Employers
  - Public Employers
  - Congress
  - Federal Agencies
  - Employment Agencies
  - Labor Organizations
- [ ] Employees and applicants of "covered employers" who have known limitations related to:
  - Pregnancy
  - Childbirth
  - Related Medical Conditions.

PWFA REASONABLE ACCOMMODATION EXAMPLES

- [ ] The ability to sit or drink water;
- [ ] Receive closer parking;
- [ ] Have flexible hours;
- [ ] Receive appropriately sized uniforms and safety apparel;
- [ ] Receive additional break time to use the bathroom, eat, and rest;
- [ ] Take leave or time off to recover from childbirth;
- [ ] Be excused from strenuous activities and/or activities that involve exposure to compounds not safe for pregnancy.
- [ ] Any other Reasonable Accommodation request unless it would cause an "undue hardship on employer's operations"—significant difficulty and expense.

UNDER THE PWFA, EMPLOYERS MUST NOT:

- [ ] Require an employee to accept an accommodation without a discussion about the accommodation
- [ ] Deny a job or other employment opportunity to a qualified EMPLOYEE
- [ ] Deny a job or other employment opportunity to a qualified APPLICANT
- [ ] Require an employee to take Leave if another reasonable accommodation can be provided that would let the employee keep working;
- [ ] Retaliate against an individual for reporting or opposing unlawful discrimination
- [ ] Interfere with any individual's rights under the PWFA.

The Pregnant Workers Fairness Act Checklist

LEGAL CONCERNS

The PWFA applies only to accommodations.

Existing laws that the EEOC enforces make it illegal to fire or otherwise discriminate against workers on the basis of pregnancy, childbirth, or related medical conditions.

The PWFA does not replace federal, state, or local laws that are more protective of workers affected by pregnancy, childbirth, or related medical conditions. It is illegal for an employer to retaliate against workers for enacting their rights under this law.

RESOURCES

Below are some federal resources you can use to understand better the PWFA and related laws.

Pregnancy Discrimination and Pregnancy-Related Disability Discrimination
> www.eeoc.gov/pregnancy-discrimination

EEOC Disability-Related Resources
> www.eeoc.gov/eeoc-disability-related-resources

Fact Sheet for Small Businesses: Pregnancy Discrimination
> www.eeoc.gov/laws/guidance/fact-sheet-small-businesses-pregnancy-discrimination

Pregnancy and Potential Intersection with Religious Discrimination
> www.eeoc.gov/laws/guidance/section-12-religious-discrimination

Helping Patients Deal with Pregnancy-Related Limitations and Restrictions at Work
> www.eeoc.gov/eeoc/publications/pregnancy_health_providers.cfm

Job Accommodation Network (JAN) on Pregnancy
> askjan.org/disabilities/Pregnancy.cfm

Some state laws provide additional protections including accommodations for pregnant workers, unpaid and paid job-protected leave, protections from discrimination, and additional rights regarding lactation.
> www.dol.gov/agencies/wb/pregnant-nursing-employment-protections

PUMP Act—Providing Urgent Maternal Protections for Nursing Mothers Act Checklist

PURPOSE

The PUMP Act was signed into law on December 29, 2022, and provides FLSA Protections for Employees to Pump Breast Milk at Work. Under the Fair Labor Standards Act (FLSA), most nursing employees have the right to reasonable break time and a place, other than a bathroom, that is shielded from view to express breast milk while at work. This updated PUMP Act expands upon the protection in the Nursing Mothers Break in the Affordable Care Act.

DEFINITIONS

FLSA: The Fair Labor Standards Act (FLSA) establishes minimum wage, overtime pay, record keeping, and youth employment standards affecting employees in the private sector and Federal, State, and local governments. Covered nonexempt workers are entitled to a minimum wage of not less than $7.25 per hour effective July 24, 2009. Overtime pay at a rate not less than one and one-half times the regular rate of pay is required after 40 hours of work in a workweek.

Non-Exempt Employees: Non-Exempt Employees are employees who are entitled to minimum wage and overtime paid at a rate of 1.5 times their regular rate of pay for all hours worked over 40 in a workweek.

Exempt Employees: The FLSA provides an exemption from both minimum wage and overtime pay for employees employed as bona fide executive, administrative, professional and outside sales employees as well as for certain computer employees. To qualify for exemption, employees generally must meet certain tests regarding their job duties and be paid on a salary basis established by the U.S. Department of Labor. There are some exceptions to the salary basis test.

PUMP Act—Providing Urgent Maternal Protections for Nursing Mothers Act Checklist

COVERED EMPLOYEES

- [ ] All employers covered by the FLSA must comply with the break time for nursing mothers provision
- [ ] Employers with 50 or less employees may not be subject to this Act if they can demonstrate that compliance with the provision would impose an undue hardship.
- [ ] Regardless of work site, all employees are counted when determining whether any exemption may apply.
- [ ] Certain employees of airlines, railroads, and motorcoach carriers are exempt from nursing employee protections but may be entitled to break and/or space protections under State or local laws.

BREAKTIME POLICIES

- [ ] Provides a reasonable amount of time to pump.
- [ ] Can be used as frequently as needed.
- [ ] Is paid or unpaid (paid not required by Federal law unless it is standard break time offered to everyone).
- [ ] If unpaid, employee completely relieved of any duties.
- [ ] Covers remote/telework employees in the same manner.
- [ ] Applies to both Exempt and Non-Exempt employees.

SPACE REQUIREMENTS

- [ ] Private space for lactating mother to pump milk is available.
- [ ] Not a bathroom
- [ ] Shielded from view
- [ ] Free from intrusion from coworkers and the public
- [ ] Can be a permanent or temporary space
- [ ] No cameras or video surveillance system
- [ ] 10 days from notification to provide an adequate space
- [ ] Break time and Private space available for up to one year after the child's birth
- [ ] Our State does/does not have a law that provides greater protections

PUMP Act—Providing Urgent Maternal Protections for Nursing Mothers Act Checklist

LEGAL CONCERNS

The PUMP Act allows a lawsuit to be filed if an Employer:

- Violated the break time requirement.
- Indicated no intention of providing private space for pumping.
- Fired or disciplined an employee for requesting break time or space.

This right is available for up to one year after the child's birth.

May or may not be compensable.

An employer may not deny a covered employee a needed break to pump.

Many employees who work in the transportation industry are exempt, including those who work as:

- airline employees
- motor carriers
- railroad employees

RESOURCES

Below are some federal resources you can use to understand better the PUMP Act and related laws.

FLSA Protections to Pump at Work
www.dol.gov/agencies/whd/pump-at-work

Frequently Asked Questions—Break Time for Nursing Mothers
www.dol.gov/agencies/whd/nursing-mothers/faq

Fact Sheet #73: FLSA Protections for Employees to Pump Breast Milk at Work
www.dol.gov/agencies/whd/fact-sheets/73-flsa-break-time-nursing-mothers

Fact Sheet #22: Hours Worked Under the Fair Labor Standards Act (FLSA)
www.dol.gov/agencies/whd/fact-sheets/22-flsa-hours-worked

Developing an AI Technology Tools Policy Checklist

PURPOSE

AI is an emerging technology tool that can serve a variety of purposes. It is a new technology and having a policy on AI tools serves as a structured and comprehensive framework to guide the development, deployment, and use of artificial intelligence (AI) technologies within an organization. This Checklist includes 15 areas for developing your own organization's AI Policy.

DEFINITIONS

AI: Artificial Intelligence

AI Tools: diverse range of software applications, frameworks, algorithms, and platforms that leverage artificial intelligence (AI) techniques to perform specific tasks or enhance decision-making. (ChatGPT, BARD, etc.)

Chatbot: A software application that uses AI to simulate conversation with users through natural language, often used for customer service, information retrieval, and interactive tasks.

Hallucinations: A situation where an AI system, particularly a language model like GPT-3, generates information that is not accurate or factual.

Algorithm: A set of rules and instructions that guide a computer program's behavior, particularly in AI and machine learning contexts where algorithms drive decision-making.

Bias in AI: When AI systems exhibit unfair or unequal behavior due to biases present in the training data, leading to unintended discriminatory outcomes.

Developing an AI Technology Tools Policy Checklist

DEFINE THE PURPOSE AND OBJECTIVES:

- [ ] Determine what AI tools and models will be utilized (ChatGPT, BARD, DALL-E, etc.)
- [ ] Consider how the selected AI models can enhance customer support, employee support, content generation, or other business processes.

LEGAL AND ETHICAL CONSIDERATIONS:

- [ ] Address potential risks of AI-generated content, such as misinformation or biased responses.
- [ ] Ensure AI-generated content complies with any laws or legal regulations and company ethical standards.
- [ ] State that current company policies regarding harassment, discrimination, and employee conduct will be in force.
- [ ] Determine how prompts using discriminatory words, hate speech, and pornographic usage of the tools will be handled.

STAKEHOLDER INVOLVEMENT:

- [ ] Involve legal, content creation, and IT/Technology teams to collectively determine use cases and guidelines.
- [ ] Obtain feedback from users and stakeholders about AI-generated content quality and appropriateness.

DATA COLLECTION AND USAGE:

- [ ] Specify data sources for training AI models and ensure they align with your data usage policies.
- [ ] Highlight transparency in disclosing when AI-generated content is being used.
- [ ] Define when and where AI generated content can be used.

DATA PRIVACY AND SECURITY:

- [ ] Detail how employee, client, and customer data is handled in interactions with AI models.
- [ ] Implement access controls to safeguard sensitive and proprietary information.
- [ ] Guidelines for sharing personal information of users.

Developing an AI Technology Tools Policy Checklist

TRANSPARENCY:

- [ ] Define how AI-generated content will be identified to end-users.
- [ ] Explore ways to provide explanations for decisions made by AI models.

BIAS MITIGATION:

- [ ] Note any potential biases in AI-generated content and develop mechanisms to mitigate them.
- [ ] Regularly review and update AI models to address new bias concerns.

ACCOUNTABILITY AND RESPONSIBILITY:

- [ ] Assign ownership of AI-generated content review and approval.
- [ ] Clearly outline roles for monitoring and addressing any content-related issues.
- [ ] Process for downloading and installing AI tools on company computers and devices.
- [ ] Define "hallucination" and error reporting procedure.
- [ ] Clarify if human oversight is required on any published or shared information.

MONITORING AND EVALUATION:

- [ ] Establish methods to monitor the quality and accuracy of AI-generated content.
- [ ] Regularly assess user satisfaction and address feedback.

HUMAN-AI COLLABORATION:

- [ ] Set guidelines for when human intervention is necessary in AI-generated interactions.
- [ ] Clarify that AI usage complements human efforts and doesn't replace necessary human involvement.

TRAINING AND EDUCATION:

- [ ] Provide training to content creators on using AI-generated content appropriately.
- [ ] Educate employees about AI's capabilities, limitations, and potential challenges.
- [ ] Training should include data protection and the risks of using confidential information.
- [ ] Process for reporting any concerns with AI Tools usage and output.

COMMUNICATION PLAN:

- [ ] Communicate to users when they are interacting with AI-generated content.
- [ ] Have a system for users to provide feedback about AI-generated interactions.

CONTINUOUS IMPROVEMENT:

- [ ] Staying updated with advancements in AI technology and assessing their potential impact on your AI policy.
- [ ] Timeframe for review and improve the policy as AI models and business needs evolve.

PILOT TESTING:

- [ ] Conduct pilot tests of AI-generated content to understand its impact and refine your policy.
- [ ] Address any unexpected outcomes that arise during testing.

CRISIS MANAGEMENT:

- [ ] Prepare strategies to address AI-generated content that may lead to misinformation or reputational harm.

Developing an AI Technology Tools Policy Checklist

LEGAL CONCERNS

COPYRIGHT AND INTELLECTUAL PROPERTY

Addressing ownership and licensing of AI-generated content to avoid intellectual property disputes and ensuring proper attribution.

PRIVACY AND DATA PROTECTION

Complying with privacy regulations, protecting user data, and establishing clear data handling practices in AI interactions.

BIAS AND DISCRIMINATION

Mitigating biases in AI outputs to prevent potential discrimination issues and potential legal consequences.

LIABILITY AND HARM

Determining liability protocols for AI-generated content causing harm and establishing mechanisms for handling legal claims.

TRANSPARENCY

Ensuring transparency in AI decision-making, and clearly outlining terms of use, limitations, and responsibilities in user agreements.

RESOURCES

Below are some resources you can use to better understand AI and related laws.

Artificial Intelligence and Algorithmic Fairness Initiative
www.eeoc.gov/ai

What the Blueprint for an AI Bill of Rights Means for Workers
blog.dol.gov/2022/10/04/what-the-blueprint-for-an-ai-bill-of-rights-means-for-workers

NLRB General Counsel Issues Memo on Unlawful Electronic Surveillance and Automated Management Practices
www.nlrb.gov/news-outreach/news-story/nlrb-general-counsel-issues-memo-on-unlawful-electronic-surveillance-and

SAMPLE Policy—The Use of Third-Party AI Tools in the Workplace

This is a sample policy based on the *Developing an AI Technology Tools Policy Checklist* from the *Ultimate Book of HR Checklists—Getting HR Right*

PURPOSE

This policy provides guidance to COMPANY employees who may want to use third party artificial intelligence tools and services to create content or perform work for COMPANY. The purpose of this policy is to ensure that AI Tools and technologies are harnessed to enhance productivity, innovation, and decision-making while adhering to ethical, legal, and security considerations including ensuring the accurate and responsible use of AI-generated information by employees to prevent potential misinformation and inaccuracies that may arise.

1. AI TOOLS DEFINED

For purposes of this policy AI Tools include third-party tools that allow a user to input a query and receive detailed results in the form of images, code, text, or other content that may have been newly generated by machine learning.

2. RESPONSIBLE USAGE OF AI TECHNOLOGIES

2.1 TRAINING AND FAMILIARIZATION

The company will provide educational materials and training to employees regarding the risks associated with using confidential information in AI tools as well as understand the capabilities, limitations, and best practices associated with these technologies. Employees will be informed of the proper practices to follow in order to protect sensitive data and comply with company policies. This training will help employees make informed decisions when using AI models like ChatGPT.

2.2 ETHICAL USE

Employees are expected to use AI technologies in a manner that respects ethical considerations, including diversity, equity, and inclusivity. AI-generated content should not promote discrimination, hate speech, or any form of harm. Any current company policies regarding harassment, discrimination, and employee conduct will be in force and cover any employee use of AI Tools.

SAMPLE Policy—The Use of Third-Party AI Tools in the Workplace Data Privacy and Security

3. RESPONSIBLE USAGE OF AI TECHNOLOGIES

3.1 DATA HANDLING

When using AI technologies, employees should ensure that sensitive and confidential data is not shared or used inappropriately this includes AI assistance tools that have recently been added to common enterprise tools like Bing, Bard, and any other internet Search Engine.

3.2 PROTECTION OF PERSONAL INFORMATION

Employees should refrain from using AI technologies to process personal information without proper authorization and compliance with relevant data protection laws.

3.3 DOWNLOADING AI TOOLS

AI Tools may not be downloaded to a COMPANY device or server without prior approval from IT.

---

4. QUALITY AND ACCURACY

4.1 VERIFICATION OF AI-GENERATED INFORMATION

AI-generated content should be carefully reviewed and validated for accuracy before being used for important decisions or external communications. Employees utilizing AI-assisted responses for job functions are required to exercise caution and verify the accuracy of the information produced by the AI before relying on it. Instances of inaccurate information produced by AI, often referred to as "hallucination," should be reported promptly to the appropriate personnel.

4.2 HUMAN OVERSIGHT AND REVIEW

Critical decisions based on AI-generated information should be subject to human oversight and confirmation. AI technologies should enhance human decision-making, not replace it.

In cases where the reliance on AI-generated information can have significant consequences, employees are directed to seek human review and confirmation for critical decisions. The company encourages a collaborative approach that combines AI efficiency with human oversight to ensure the quality and accuracy of information.

5. OWNERSHIP OF AI-GENERATED CONTENT

Employees should be aware that the ownership of content generated by AI technologies remains with the organization.

6. EXPOSURE OF CONFIDENTIAL OR TRADE SECRET INFORMATION

6.1 PROTECTION OF CONFIDENTIAL INFORMATION

Employees are prohibited from using AI tools with access to company confidential, proprietary, or trade secret information. This includes sensitive data, customer information, and any content that may be contractually bound by non-disclosure agreements.

6.2 LIMITING DATA INCLUSION

Employees are advised not to include any proprietary or confidential information in AI prompts or inputs. The use of such information in AI-generated responses may lead to unintentional exposure and disclosure, which could compromise the company's interests.

7. INFRINGEMENT OF THIRD-PARTY INTELLECTUAL PROPERTY RIGHTS

7.1 RESPECT FOR INTELLECTUAL PROPERTY

Employees are required to respect copyright, trademark, and other intellectual property rights when using AI applications. The use of AI-generated content that may infringe on third-party rights is strictly prohibited.

7.2 LIMITATIONS ON CONTENT USAGE

Employees should avoid using AI-generated content that may include copyrighted or trademarked material unless they have obtained proper permissions. This applies to any content used for company purposes or in external communications. Any content created by AI should be reviewed for originality and compliance with copyright laws.

SAMPLE Policy—The Use of Third-Party AI Tools in the Workplace Data Privacy and Security

8. USAGE OF RESULTS

No content from any AI Tools may be used in any <COMPANY> products or materials that could be provided to customer or partners (training materials, documentation, code, etc.) without proper permission and approval, including results in the form of images (pictures, gifs, videos, etc.). Without approvals, AI generated content may only be used internally, and not shared with customers, partners, or the general public.

9. COMPLIANCE AND ENFORCEMENT

9.1 POLICY ADHERENCE

Employees are expected to adhere to all aspects of this policy. Failure to comply with the guidelines may result in disciplinary actions, including loss of AI tool access or other appropriate measures.

9.2 REPORTING CONCERNS

Employees should report any concerns related to the use of AI technologies to their supervisors or the designated responsible personnel.

10. POLICY REVIEW AND EXCEPTIONS

This comprehensive policy will be reviewed periodically to ensure its relevance and effectiveness in addressing the evolving landscape of AI technologies.

Given that the landscape of AI tools is changing rapidly, updates to this policy may happen frequently period to request any exceptions to this policy please contact [insert company contact here].

Company Holiday Party Legal Considerations Checklist

PURPOSE

The company holiday party is a time of celebration and camaraderie, but it also presents various legal considerations that must be addressed. This checklist serves as a structured framework to guide the planning, organization, and execution of company holiday parties. It outlines key legal aspects to ensure a safe and enjoyable event for all attendees.

DEFINITIONS

Alcohol Consumption: The responsible provision of alcoholic beverages at the event, including measures such as drink tickets and monitoring consumption to prevent excessive drinking.

Harassment and Discrimination: Inclusive and respectful behavior that upholds anti-harassment and anti-discrimination policies, fostering an environment free from harassment or discrimination based on protected characteristics.

Workplace Safety: Ensuring the safety of all attendees at the event venue, taking precautions for activities with potential safety risks, and obtaining necessary waivers for risky activities.

Overtime and Wage Laws: Compliance with wage and hour laws, including compensation for non-exempt employees attending during work hours.

Religious Accommodations: Consideration of diverse religious and cultural backgrounds, offering alternative events or activities to respect different beliefs.

Company Holiday Party Legal Considerations Checklist

ALCOHOL CONSUMPTION:

- ☐ Implement responsible alcohol service measures, such as drink tickets and monitoring consumption.
- ☐ Hire a professional bartender or bartending service.
- ☐ Arrange transportation alternatives for attendees who are intoxicated.
- ☐ Avoid serving alcohol to visibly intoxicated individuals.

HARASSMENT AND DISCRIMINATION:

- ☐ Reinforce anti-harassment and anti-discrimination policies before the event.
- ☐ Create an inclusive and respectful atmosphere that considers diverse cultural and religious backgrounds.
- ☐ Address any inappropriate behavior promptly and according to company policies

WORKPLACE SAFETY:

- ☐ Ensure the event venue is safe for all attendees.
- ☐ Take necessary precautions for activities with potential safety risks.
- ☐ Obtain signed waivers for activities that involve risk.

OVERTIME AND WAGE LAWS:

- ☐ Pay non-exempt employees that are on "party committee' and also setting up and cleaning up.
- ☐ Determine if non-exempt employees attending during work hours should be compensated.
- ☐ Comply with wage and hour laws in relation to attendance and compensation.

RELIGIOUS ACCOMMODATIONS:

- ☐ Consider alternative events or activities for employees with different celebrations.
- ☐ Reconsider décor regarding religious-themed items.
- ☐ Ensure the holiday party is respectful and inclusive of all beliefs.

PRIVACY CONSIDERATIONS:

- [ ] Obtain consent from individuals before taking and sharing event photos.
- [ ] Respect attendees' privacy when using images on company platforms.

SOCIAL MEDIA POLICIES:

- [ ] Remind attendees to follow company social media guidelines during the event.
- [ ] Encourage responsible social media use to maintain the company's reputation.

GIFT EXCHANGES:

- [ ] Set clear guidelines for appropriate gifts during any gift exchange activities.
- [ ] Prevent offensive or inappropriate gift exchanges to maintain a positive atmosphere.

LIABILITY AND INSURANCE:

- [ ] Confirm that liability insurance covers the event and potential accidents or incidents.
- [ ] Understand the extent of coverage and how to report any issues.

TRANSPORTATION SAFETY:

- [ ] Ensure safe transportation arrangements if applicable.
- [ ] Provide alternative transportation options for attendees who cannot or should not drive.

Company Holiday Party Legal Considerations Checklist

LEGAL CONCERNS

ALCOHOL CONSUMPTION

Risk of accidents and injuries due to excessive drinking. Liability for serving alcohol to visibly intoxicated individuals.

HARASSMENT AND DISCRIMINATION

Potential lawsuits for failing to prevent harassment or discrimination at the event. Damage to company reputation and employee morale.

WORKPLACE SAFETY

Injuries or accidents at the event may lead to legal claims. Negligence claims if proper safety precautions are not taken.

OVERTIME AND WAGE LAWS

Non-compliance with wage and hour laws can result in legal actions. Claims for unpaid work hours during the event.

RELIGIOUS ACCOMMODATIONS

Discrimination claims if employees' religious needs are not respected. Legal consequences for excluding certain religious groups.

PRIVACY CONSIDERATIONS

Breach of privacy claims if event photos are shared without consent. Potential legal issues related to unauthorized image use.

SOCIAL MEDIA POLICIES

Damage to the company's online reputation and brand. Legal issues arising from inappropriate social media posts.

GIFT EXCHANGES

Complaints or legal actions related to offensive or inappropriate gifts. Negative impact on workplace relationships and morale.

LIABILITY AND INSURANCE

Lack of coverage for accidents or incidents during the event. Financial exposure for the company.

TRANSPORTATION SAFETY

Liability for accidents or injuries during transportation. Legal consequences for not providing safe transportation options.

RESOURCES

Below are some websites with some related information.

U.S. Equal Employment Opportunity Commission
www.eeoc.gov/employers/small-business/small-business-toolbox—Small Business Toolbox

U.S. Department of Labor
blog.dol.gov/2021/11/23/know-your-rights-this-holiday-season—Know Your Rights This Holiday Season

Difficult Conversation Checklists

PURPOSE

One of the hardest things we must do as Human Resources Practitioners is to have difficult conversations. This could be telling an employee they are not meeting organizational expectations. It could be telling a leader what they are doing is possibly illegal. It could be telling a coworker that they are being disrespectful to us. This difficult conversation checklist is a guide to having hard conversations in the workplace. There is no formula for difficult conversations, as situations can vary. However, there is a pattern that, when followed, helps us be better prepared to have those conversations.

NOTES

Communication is critical in the workplace; however, many conversations go unsaid because they are difficult for either the initiator or the subject. However, when we have difficult conversations, they build stronger relationships, increase productivity, and help us find common ground.

The Team at HR Stories has developed a workshop, Difficult Conversations at Work, to teach teams how difficult conversations are necessary and help organizations thrive. If you are interested, please contact The Team at HR Stories at email@teamathrstories.com and we will get you on the schedule.

Difficult Conversation Checklists

PREPARING FOR THE CONVERSATION

☐ **Describe Your Conversation Partner**

- Tenure with the Organization
- Authority
- Experience in their role
- Points of Connection with You
- Expertise
- Emotional Competency
- Cultural Background
- Values

☐ **Define the Issue You Want to Address**

- Situation: A one-time offense that is out of expected norms.
- Pattern: A repeated pattern of behaviors that have been discussed, and nothing has changed.
- Relationship: The string of behaviors that has started to diminish the trust or bond of the relationship.
- Describe the outcome you want from the conversation.

☐ **Explore the Issue In More Detail**

- Motivational Issue: They are motivated to behave this way either by self-enjoyment, peer pressure, or systemically.
- Capability: They are incapable of behaving to expectations because of a lack of knowledge, others are holding them back, or there is friction in the system.

☐ **Prepare Ourselves for the Conversation**

- Change mindset from "Difficult" to "Necessary" Conversation
- Plan out what you will say, but don't script it
- Practice or Role Play
- Prepare to listen to their perspective
- Know your boundaries
- Have a resolution in mind, but be flexible

Difficult Conversation Checklists

☐ **Create Conversational Safety**
- Enhance psychological safety for yourself and others
- Ask—"Is there a shared purpose?"—"Do they feel that you are working towards the same shared purpose?"
- Ask—"Is there mutual respect?"—Do they feel that you mutually respect each other?

☐ **Having the Conversation**
- Define the missed expectation
- Anticipate their point of view
- Build Safety for you and them
- Share your story
- Discuss the impact on you, the team, and the organization
- Ask a question
- Listen. Be curious.
- Explore the Issue
- Solve it together
- Gain Commitment

☐ **After the Conversation**
- Meet Commitments
- Check-up: Follow up with the other person to make sure they are meeting expectations
- Recognize and Reward met expectations
- Celebrate

Difficult Conversation Checklists

LEGAL CONCERNS

Although there are no employment laws regarding difficult conversations, if you don't properly handle them, they can lead to legal concerns. For instance, if you have a difficult conversation with an employee and you or they have an emotional response, this could lead to legal action.

RESOURCES

Kerry Patterson, Joseph Grenny, Ron McMillan, and Al Switzler, *Crucial Conversations: Tools for Talking When Stakes are High, Third Edition,* (New York: McGraw-Hill, 2021)

Kerry Patterson, Joseph Grenny, Ron McMillan, and Al Switzler, *Crucial Confrontations: Tools for Resolving Broken Promises, Violated Expectations, and Bad Behavior* (New York: McGraw-Hill, 2004)

Melody Standford Martin, *Brave Talk: Building Resilient Relationships in the Face of Conflict* (Cambridge: Broadleaf Press, 2020)

The Team at HR Stories
    www.teamathrstories.com

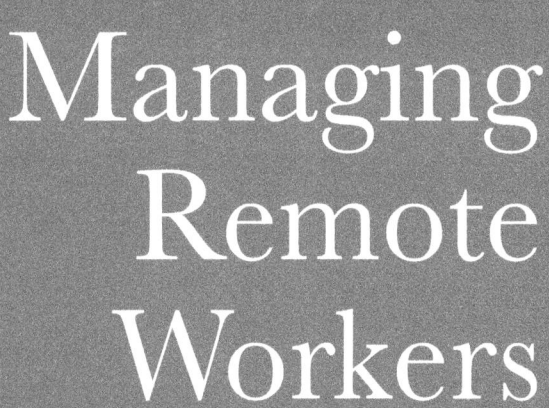

Managing Remote Workers

Remote Teams Policy Checklist

PURPOSE

It is a best practice to have a formalized remote work policy to clarify any items and align expectations between the employee and employer. When drafting a policy for your remote/telework/work-from-home employees, this *Ultimate HR Checklist* provides considerations to include in your policy document.

DEFINITIONS

Remote Work: In this *Ultimate HR Checklist*, we use the term remote work to mean work from home, work from anywhere, telework, virtual, or hybrid workplace. It is essential for organizations to clearly state what their remote work policy is.

Remote Teams Policy Checklist

- [ ] What types of jobs are allowed to be remote/telework
- [ ] Eligibility guidelines and criteria for employees who want to work remotely
- [ ] Selection criteria for choosing eligible employees
- [ ] List of required equipment, supplies, and internet access
- [ ] Contingency/backup plan when company equipment breaks down or needs "troubleshooting."
- [ ] Protocol to return equipment and property upon termination

CONSIDERATION ITEMS TO INCLUDE IN YOUR POLICY

- [ ] Is employee allowed to work on public Wi-Fi or in co-working spaces (e.g., coffee shops)
- [ ] Forwarding company work to personal computers and printers (allowed or not allowed)
- [ ] Employees must safeguard and protect against unauthorized or accidental access, use, modification, destruction, or disclosure of company data
- [ ] All obligations, responsibilities, and conditions of employment remain the same
- [ ] Employee must be able to carry out the same performance duties as in the office
- [ ] Hours of work defined
- [ ] Any expectations for remote employees to work on-premises if requested
- [ ] All current company policies still in place, including but NOT limited to:
    - At-Will statement
    - Attendance
    - Social Media
    - Dress Code
    - Harassment
    - Confidentiality
- [ ] Hourly/Non-exempt employees are not to work off the clock
- [ ] Hourly/Non-exempt employees must clock in/out—account for all hours worked
- [ ] Employees must report any work-related injuries
- [ ] Company has the right to cancel or suspend the program
- [ ] Employee compensation, benefits, work status, and work responsibilities will not change due to participation in the program
- [ ] Except as required by law, a statement about out-of-pocket expenses for office supplies and equipment
- [ ] Employee Agreement with itemized costs of company-owned equipment

Remote Teams Policy Checklist

LEGAL CONCERNS

STATE AND LOCAL LAWS

Each state where you have employees working will have different laws and regulations that you will need to follow in regards to taxes, leave policies, etc.

RESOURCES

Multistate Compliance for Employers With Out-of-State Remote Employee
www.natlawreview.com/article/multistate-compliance-employers-out-state-remote-employee

Article: So Your Employee Wants To Work Remotely Out Of State?
www.jdsupra.com/legalnews/so-your-employee-wants-to-work-remotely-7417549

The Ultimate Guide to Working From Home
www.investopedia.com/personal-finance/work-from-home-guide

Remote/Teleworker Agreement Checklist

PURPOSE

If you have remote workers or any type of dispersed workforce, a best practice will be to have an agreement for them to sign to ensure organization and employee expectations are transparent. It will also formalize the work arrangement and clear up any misconceptions. In this *Ultimate HR Checklist*, you will find some items to consider for your agreement.

DEFINITIONS

Remote Work: In this *Ultimate HR Checklist*, we use the term remote work to mean work from home, work from anywhere, telework, virtual, or hybrid workplace. It is important for organizations to clearly state what their remote work policy is.

Remote/Teleworker Agreement Checklist

- [ ] The agreed-upon times of work hours should be specified
- [ ] Outline how work hours will be tracked and reported
- [ ] For hourly/non-exempt employees—no off-the-clock working is allowed
- [ ] The location in the home that the employee agrees to work from
- [ ] How and to whom the employee reports work-related injuries
- [ ] Internet speed requirements and other related standards
- [ ] The type of monitoring that may occur and that there is no expectation of privacy
- [ ] Childcare arrangements during work time
- [ ] Itemized list and costs of company-owned equipment
- [ ] Return of equipment, files, and any other company property upon termination
- [ ] What duties, obligations, and responsibilities remain the same or are different
- [ ] Productivity expectations
- [ ] Reimbursement of any expenses that are or are not covered
- [ ] Rate of compensation—if it is adjusted based on the remote work arrangement
- [ ] Signature and date lines for employee and manager
- [ ] Privacy and Client confidentiality expectations
- [ ] That all other Human Resources policies are still in effect (unless otherwise noted)
- [ ] That employee may be asked to travel and attend in-office meetings or other events
- [ ] That remote work/telecommuting arrangement can be canceled at any time
- [ ] Computer security and virus protection protocols
- [ ] If remote work in public places (coffee shops, libraries, etc.) is allowed or not
- [ ] That at-will employment is still in place (for most states)
- [ ] Clarification if forwarding work to personal computer or printer is allowed
- [ ] Communication, responsiveness, and availability expectations

Remote/Teleworker Agreement Checklist

LEGAL CONCERNS

Each state where you have employees working will have different laws and regulations that you will need to follow in regards to taxes, leave policies, etc.

RESOURCES

Multistate Compliance for Employers With Out-of-State Remote Employee
www.natlawreview.com/article/multistate-compliance-employers-out-state-remote-employee

Article: So Your Employee Wants To Work Remotely Out Of State?
www.jdsupra.com/legalnews/so-your-employee-wants-to-work-remotely-7417549

The Ultimate Guide to Working From Home
www.investopedia.com/personal-finance/work-from-home-guide

Home Office Employee Readiness Checklist

PURPOSE

More and more employees are working from home. Employers must make sure that employees are prepared to work from home. Use this *Ultimate HR Checklist* for employees that want to work remotely from a Home Office. These are questions to ask them which will reveal preparedness and to ensure they are set up for success.

DEFINITIONS

Work from Home: Work from home is defined as when an employee works from their primary residence.

Remote Work: In this *Ultimate HR Checklist*, we use the term remote work to mean work from home, work from anywhere, telework, virtual, or hybrid workplace. It is important for organizations to clearly state what their remote work policy is.

Home Office Employee Readiness Checklist

- [ ] Are you happy spending long periods on your own?
- [ ] Do you consider yourself self-disciplined and self-motivated?
- [ ] Are you confident working without supervision?
- [ ] Can you be comfortable communicating with colleagues via email, chat, video conference, etc., instead of face to face?
- [ ] Will telecommuting help you achieve the work-life balance you want?
- [ ] Do you have a quiet area or separate private room for conducting business?
- [ ] Can you create and maintain an atmosphere that is free from interruptions?
- [ ] How will you handle common distractions that might occur?
  - Pets
  - Children
  - Delivery people
- [ ] What type of internet access do you have?
- [ ] How will you safeguard confidential info; do you have a secured locked cabinet available to only you?
- [ ] Have you notified your insurance company to confirm there are no issues with your policy and working from home?
- [ ] Will you need any accommodations to work remotely from home?
- [ ] Do you understand the expectations for the work-from-home position?
- [ ] Do you have the necessary equipment to conduct business virtually?
  - Phone
  - Camera
  - Microphone
  - Lighting
- [ ] Are you trained in our platforms for conducting business virtually, and do you require any additional training?

Home Office Employee Readiness Checklist

LEGAL CONCERNS

Each state where you have employees working will have different laws and regulations that you will need to follow in regards to taxes, leave policies, etc.

RESOURCES

Multistate Compliance for Employers With Out-of-State Remote Employee
www.natlawreview.com/article/multistate-compliance-employers-out-state-remote-employee

Article: So Your Employee Wants To Work Remotely Out Of State?
www.jdsupra.com/legalnews/so-your-employee-wants-to-work-remotely-7417549

The Ultimate Guide to Working From Home
www.investopedia.com/personal-finance/work-from-home-guide

Remote Employee Satisfaction Questions Checklist

PURPOSE

This *Ultimate HR Checklist* of questions will help you evaluate the health and satisfaction of your remote workforce. Use them in group meetings to elicit discussion or check-in with individual employees during one-on-one sessions.

DEFINITIONS

Work from Home: Work from home is defined as when an employee works from their primary residence.

Remote Work: In this *Ultimate HR Checklist*, we use the term remote work to mean work from home, work from anywhere, telework, virtual, or hybrid workplace. It is important for organizations to clearly state what their remote work policy is.

Remote Employee Satisfaction Questions Checklist

☐ Are your goals and objectives for the week clear?

☐ Do you know what is expected of you every day?

☐ How has it been sticking to a work schedule as a remote employee?

☐ Do your remote work tools (e.g., VPN, remote work access, communication tools) help you be more productive or less?

- If less, why?
- What necessary tools are missing, if any?

☐ Do you feel as effective at home as at the office?

- What is the biggest thing you currently struggle with while working from home?

☐ What additional support is needed from management?

☐ Do you feel that you can easily reach/connect with colleagues?

☐ Are you feeling more in the loop or out of the loop?

- What would make you feel in the loop?

☐ Do you think you are getting enough interaction with colleagues?

- How can interaction with your colleagues be improved?

☐ Is the work from home policy is clear to you?

- If not, how can we improve upon it?

☐ Overall, what improvement suggestions do you have so that our organization can communicate more efficiently?

☐ Have you been able to create a hard line between work and home?

☐ How do you feel about your ability to work from home?

☐ How can your work from home experience be improved?

Remote Employee Satisfaction Questions Checklist

LEGAL CONCERNS

Each state where you have employees working will have different laws and regulations that you will need to follow in regards to taxes, leave policies, etc.

The other concern that is being raised is discrimination and harassment. These questions will help the employer discover if an employee is being harassed or unintentionally being discriminated against.

RESOURCES

Multistate Compliance for Employers With Out-of-State Remote Employee
  www.natlawreview.com/article/multistate-compliance-employers-out-state-remote-employee

Article: So Your Employee Wants To Work Remotely Out Of State?
  www.jdsupra.com/legalnews/so-your-employee-wants-to-work-remotely-7417549

The Ultimate Guide to Working From Home
  www.investopedia.com/personal-finance/work-from-home-guide

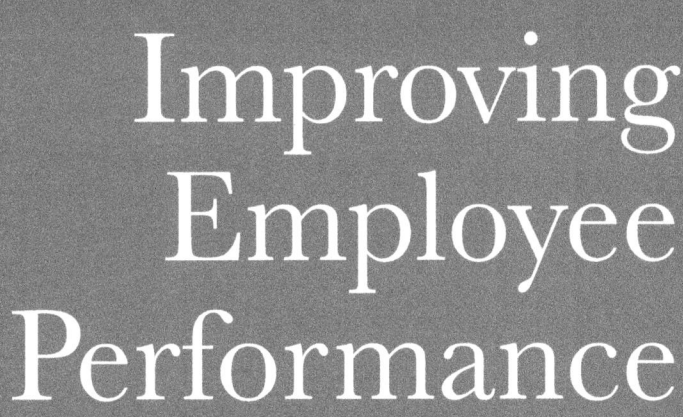

Improving Employee Performance

Performance Management Checklist

PURPOSE

One of the most critical roles of the Human Resources Department is to create a work environment in which all employees can excel. This is accomplished by developing a structured performance management system that treats all employees equally and improves their understanding of their expectations. More than just an Annual Review, a Performance Management System harnesses all of the available tools (reviews/appraisals, SMART GOALS, and the PIP) to create a structured employee performance and improvement approach.

DEFINITIONS

Employ: By statutory definition, the term "employ" includes "to suffer or permit to work." The workweek ordinarily includes all time during which an employee is necessarily required to be on the employer's premises, on duty, or at a prescribed workplace.

"Workday," in general, means the period between the time on any particular day when such employee commences their "principal activity" and the time on that day at which they cease such principal activity or activities; therefore, the workday may be longer than the employee's scheduled shift, hours, tour of duty, or production line time.

Performance: Performance is how effective an employee is at meeting their job expectations.

Performance Management Checklist

- [ ] Develop organizational competencies
- [ ] Create competency requirements based on level
- [ ] Work with managers to define expectations for all employees based on job descriptions
    - Desired outcomes for the role
    - Define tasks and responsibilities to reach desired outcomes
    - Discuss behavioral norms based on the company's competencies
- [ ] Review expectations with employees
- [ ] Set goals using the SMART Goal Checklist
- [ ] Manager monitors and tracks performance
- [ ] The manager holds the employee accountable for expectations
- [ ] The manager documents performance
- [ ] Save the document in the personnel file
- [ ] The manager offers support to improve employees' performance.
    - What knowledge do they need to do their job well?
    - What skills do they need to do their job well?
    - What systems do they need to do their job well?
    - What guidance do they need to do their job well?
- [ ] If necessary, use the Performance Improvement Plan Checklist.

Performance Management Checklist

LEGAL CONCERNS

DISCRIMINATION

Under Title VII of the Civil Rights Act of 1964, organizations must treat employees equally and not discriminate against them based on the defined protected classes.

RESOURCES

Job Description Checklist (page 58)

Performance Improvement PIP Form (page 233)

SMART Goals (page 236)

Performance Improvement PIP Form

PURPOSE

A Performance Improvement Process form (PIP) is a framework for improving an employee's substandard job performance. Utilizing the format below, a PIP allows a manager to be particular with expectations on areas employees must improve. The PIP is more effective if approached from an ongoing time-specific perspective rather than a "once and done" event. Setting up a weekly, bi-weekly, or monthly meeting to evaluate the progress of the PIP is essential to a successful implementation.

DEFINITIONS

Employ: By statutory definition, the term "employ" includes "to suffer or permit to work." The workweek ordinarily includes all time during which an employee is necessarily required to be on the employer's premises, on duty, or at a prescribed workplace.

"Workday," in general, means the period between the time on any particular day when such employee commences their "principal activity" and the time on that day at which they cease such principal activity or activities; therefore, the workday may be longer than the employee's scheduled shift, hours, tour of duty, or production line time.

Performance: Performance is how effective an employee is at meeting the expectations of their job.

Performance Improvement PIP Form

EMPLOYEE NAME: _____

DATE: _____

EMPLOYEE'S ID#: _____

POSITION: _____

DEPARTMENT: _____

TASK	EXPECTED OUTCOME	EVALUATION	FOCUS
Tasks that employee needs to do their job well.	What are the desired results for this task?	Meets/Below/Above	High/Low

THE ORGANIZATION WILL PROVIDE ADDITIONAL SUPPORT TO HELP THE EMPLOYEE ACHIEVE EXPECTATIONS

Skill Building: _____
_____
_____

Training: _____
_____

Resources: _____
_____

Performance Improvement PIP Form

LEGAL CONCERNS

DISCRIMINATION

Under Title VII of the Civil Rights Act of 1964, organizations must treat employees equally and not discriminate against them based on the defined protected classes.

RESOURCES

Job Description Checklist (page 58)

Performance Improvement PIP Form (page 233)

SMART Goals (page 236)

SMART Goals

PURPOSE

The SMART Goals format is a specific way to capture goals for your team members. Research has shown that those individuals who set specific goals are much more likely to complete them. A SMART goal is a goal that is Specific, Measurable, Attainable, Relevant, and Timely. This SMART goals format can be used in a variety of ways during the employment process to provide focus and clarity to employees.

DEFINITIONS

Employ: By statutory definition, the term "employ" includes "to suffer or permit to work." The workweek ordinarily includes all time during which an employee is necessarily required to be on the employer's premises, on duty, or at a prescribed workplace.

"Workday," in general, means the period between the time on any particular day when such employee commences their "principal activity" and the time on that day at which they cease such principal activity or activities; therefore, the workday may be longer than the employee's scheduled shift, hours, tour of duty, or production line time.

Performance: Performance is how effective an employee is at meeting the expectations of their job.

SMART Goals

SPECIFIC

Be as detailed as possible about what you want to accomplish. There is a big difference between I want to lose weight and I want to lose 13 pounds. Alternatively, in the business sense, there is a big difference between selling more products to increase our market share by fifteen percent in all metropolitan areas with a population of between 100,000 and 250,000

MEASURABLE

Peter Drucker said it best, "If you can't measure it, you can't improve it." Almost everything can be measured, so take time to figure out what measurement you are going to use to decide whether you have met your goal or not.

ATTAINABLE

Is this a goal that you can attain? It is easy to say I want to be a professional video gamer. Still, it is possible in the timeline you have given yourself. It might be necessary to create smaller milestones instead of going for the big goal. For instance, at work, you might want to be the number one cupcake seller in your town, but since you started your business, you have only sold 25,000 cupcakes while the number one producer is selling 250,000 cupcakes. Instead, your goal may be to increase cupcakes sold by fifteen percent for the next five years.

RELEVANT

Is your goal relevant to your significant purpose? At work, this will mean your objectives are related to your organizational goals. Let's say you are a baker at the above cupcake company. Your goal is to produce more soft pretzels; this would not be relevant to the organizational purpose of selling fifteen percent more cupcakes per year.

TIMELY

Have you set a time to complete your goal? If there is no timeline, you are more likely not to achieve your goal. Also, make sure that your goal can meet your destination within the time frame.

SMART Goals

TURN YOUR GOAL INTO A SMART GOAL

S	SPECIFIC	
M	MEASURABLE	
A	ATTAINABLE	
R	RELEVANT	
T	TIMELY	

Termination Checklist

PURPOSE

Even if done correctly, the termination process is one that can leave employers of all sizes legally exposed and vulnerable. That is why it is essential to have a Checklist to ensure all steps are consistently followed. The Checklist below should be followed for any voluntary or involuntary terminations.

DEFINITIONS

Termination: **Termination of employment** or **separation of employment** is an employee's departure from a job and the end of an employee's duration with an employer. Termination may be voluntary on the employee's part, or it may be at the hands of the employer, often in the form of dismissal (firing) or a layoff. Dismissal or firing is usually thought to be the fault of the employee. In contrast, a layoff is generally done for business reasons (for instance, a business slowdown or an economic downturn) outside the employee's performance.

—en.wikipedia.org/wiki/Termination_of_employment

Termination Checklist

VOLUNTARY TERMINATION

- [ ] Accept resignation letter—confirm last day.
- [ ] Schedule exit interview.
- [ ] Complete exit interview. (See exit interview format.)

INVOLUNTARY TERMINATION

- [ ] Hold termination meeting.
  - Prepare
  - Review reason for consistency
  - No surprises
  - Have witness attend meeting
  - Be concise
  - Treat with dignity
- [ ] Provide employee with termination letter.
- [ ] Provide employee with severance agreement if laid off.
- [ ] Review warn/owbpa if applicable.

PREPARING FOR TERMINATION

- [ ] Review policies for consistency.
- [ ] Review employee files for post-employment obligations (non-competition agreements, confidentiality agreements, company equipment policies, etc.). Provide a copy for the employee.
- [ ] Alert security—remove access upon termination.
- [ ] Alert IT—terminate access upon termination.
- [ ] Alert Payroll to process final check. (Discuss PTO benefits.)
- [ ] Schedule the termination meeting—use a conference room.

TERMINATION

- [ ] State the reason the employee is being terminated.
- [ ] Listen, but don't prolong the conversation.
- [ ] Review benefit information.
    - Termination/Continuation of employment insurance benefits such as COBRA, Life Insurance, etc.
    - Review Vacation/Sick/PTO Policy and review the status with the employee.
- [ ] Review Company Equipment Policy and ask for it to be returned to the company.
- [ ] Hand Final Paycheck or provide the date when it will be received.
- [ ] Escort them from the building.

AFTER TERMINATION (VOLUNTARY AND INVOLUNTARY)

- [ ] Pull employee file—move to terminated employee files.
- [ ] Note date on I-9 Form.
- [ ] Arrange for the employee to pick up personal belongings or have them shipped.
- [ ] Confirm that email account/computer access is disabled.
- [ ] Remove employee's name from group lists.
- [ ] Disable phone extension.
- [ ] Confirm that employee doesn't have access to the building or secure areas.
- [ ] Have manager clean out workstation.
- [ ] Make sure the following have been collected. (Keys, ID Card, Access Cards, Company equipment, Uniforms, Tools)
- [ ] Meet with team to answer any questions (keep confidentiality).

Termination Checklist

LEGAL CONCERNS

TITLE VII OF THE CIVIL RIGHTS ACT OF 1964

Title VII prohibits employment discrimination based on race, color, religion, sex, and national origin. All employers in the United States with fifteen or more employees for each working day in each of twenty or more calendar weeks in the current or preceding calendar year.

- [ ] Discrimination can happen numerous times of the employee life cycle, including;
  - job advertisements and postings
  - employment references, job referrals
  - discipline and discharge
  - application and hiring practices
  - job assignments and promotions
  - reasonable accommodations and disability
  - pay and benefits
  - recruitment practices
  - training and apprenticeship programs.

Employers must be careful not to unintentionally or intentionally discriminate against their employees and candidates applying for jobs.

Please make sure you review your state law for how you have to pay an employee when they are terminated from your employment.

DISCRIMINATION LAWS INCLUDE BUT ARE NOT LIMITED TO:

- [ ] Civil Rights Act of 1964–Title VII
- [ ] Americans with Disabilities Act
- [ ] Age Discrimination in Employment Act
- [ ] Pregnancy Act of 1978
- [ ] Equal Pay Act of 1963
- [ ] Genetic Information Non-discrimination Act (GINA)
- [ ] Vietnam Era Veteran's Readjustment Act (VEVRA)
- [ ] Don't forget to familiarize yourself with state and local employment laws. The other legal concern is inconsistency in how your exit interviews are handled.

NOTE: Do not forget to review your state and local leave laws.

EMPLOYEE-AT-WILL

In all states except Montana, there is a statute called Employment-at-Will, which says that the employer or the employee can sever the relationship for any reason with or without notice (as long as it is legal).

DOCUMENTATION AND CONSISTENCY

Two critical aspects of managing our employees are documentation and consistency. We need to document the employee's performance and actions throughout the employee life cycle. So if there is an instance where the company is audited or winds up in court, the employer has a detailed explanation through documentation of how the employee was treated. On the other hand, consistency is also important because if an employer is not consistent with how they treat their employees, they may inadvertently discriminate against an employee.

RESOURCES

How to Fire Employees After They Filed a Claim With the EEOC
smallbusiness.chron.com/fire-employees-after-filed-claim-eeoc-12023.html

U.S. Equal Employment Opportunity Commission
www.eeoc.gov/employers/small-business/7-i-need-discipline-or-fire-employee

U.S. Department of Labor
www.dol.gov/general/topic/termination

Exit Interview Questionnaire

PURPOSE

The purpose of the exit interview is to understand better why an employee is leaving and what adjustments you can make in the future to either retain or attract employees. It can also help you find illegal or harmful practices that impact your coworkers. In most cases, the employee is more open about their opinions and thoughts about the workplace during an exit interview when their job is no longer on the line.

DEFINITIONS

Employ: By statutory definition, the term "employ" includes "to suffer or permit to work." The workweek ordinarily includes all time during which an employee is necessarily required to be on the employer's premises, on duty, or at a prescribed workplace.

"Workday," in general, means the period between the time on any particular day when such employee commences their "principal activity" and the time on that day at which they cease such principal activity or activities; therefore, the workday may be longer than the employee's scheduled shift, hours, tour of duty, or production line time.

Exit Interview Questionnaire

1. What triggered you to start searching for a new job?
2. Did your manager give you the support you needed to do your job well?
3. What did you like most about your job?
4. What did you like least about your job?
5. What was your biggest challenge at work?
6. How has the job changed since you were hired?
7. How did the organization value you during your tenure here?
8. What constructive criticism would you offer the organization?
9. What is the organization doing right?
10. What changes would be necessary for you to stay with the organization?
11. What words would you use to describe your experience at the organization?
12. What concerns have you brought to your management team's attention? How was it received?
13. If you have a new job, what was the deciding factor?
14. How satisfied were you with your present manager? What changes would you like to see in their performance?
15. What support (knowledge, skill-building, systems, or guidance) should we be offering your team?
16. Would you consider working here in the future?

Exit Interview Questionnaire

LEGAL CONCERNS

TITLE VII OF THE CIVIL RIGHTS ACT OF 1964

Title VII prohibits employment discrimination based on race, color, religion, sex, and national origin. All employers in the United States with fifteen or more employees for each working day in each of twenty or more calendar weeks in the current or preceding calendar year.

☐ Discrimination can happen numerous times of the employee life cycle, including;
- job advertisements and postings
- employment references, job referrals
- discipline and discharge
- application and hiring practices
- job assignments and promotions
- reasonable accommodations and disability
- pay and benefits
- recruitment practices
- training and apprenticeship programs.

Employers must be careful not to unintentionally or intentionally discriminate against their employees and candidates applying for jobs.

DISCRIMINATION LAWS INCLUDE BUT ARE NOT LIMITED TO:

☐ Pregnant Workers Fairness Act
☐ Civil Rights Act of 1964–Title VII
☐ Americans with Disabilities Act
☐ Age Discrimination in Employment Act
☐ Pregnancy Act of 1978
☐ Equal Pay Act of 1963
☐ Genetic Information Non-discrimination Act (GINA)
☐ Vietnam Era Veteran's Readjustment Act (VEVRA)

NOTE: Do not forget to familiarize yourself with state and local employment laws.

The other legal concern is inconsistency in how your exit interviews are handled. For instance, do not just do exit interviews for people under the age of forty or any particular protected classes.

RESOURCES

See Stay interviews

Using a Performance Improvement Plan (PIP)

BEFORE THE PIP IS PUT INTO PLACE

- [ ] Set and communicate expectations with employee
- [ ] Observe and evaluate the employee (use other's perspectives to get the complete performance picture)
- [ ] Coach employee (see Coaching Steps)
- [ ] Provide the necessary support to help the employee meet job expectations (knowledge, skill-building, systems, and resources)
- [ ] If the employee continues not to meet expectations—create a Performance Improvement Plan

INCLUDED IN THE PIP

- [ ] Employee's Name
- [ ] Position and Department
- [ ] Date
- [ ] Role Expectations as defined in the job description. Focusing on the essential aspect of the job.
- [ ] Where the employee rates in each area
- [ ] Note which areas need improvement
- [ ] Action Plan including a timeline

Using a Performance Improvement Plan (PIP)

LEGAL CONCERNS

TITLE VII OF THE CIVIL RIGHTS ACT OF 1964

Title VII prohibits employment discrimination based on race, color, religion, sex, and national origin. All employers in the United States with fifteen or more employees for each working day in each of twenty or more calendar weeks in the current or preceding calendar year.

- [ ] Discrimination can happen numerous times of the employee life cycle, including;
    - job advertisements and postings
    - employment references, job referrals
    - discipline and discharge
    - application and hiring practices
    - job assignments and promotions
    - reasonable accommodations and disability
    - pay and benefits
    - recruitment practices
    - training and apprenticeship programs.

Employers must be careful not to unintentionally or intentionally discriminate against their employees and candidates applying for jobs.

DISCRIMINATION LAWS INCLUDE BUT ARE NOT LIMITED TO:

- [ ] Civil Rights Act of 1964–Title VII
- [ ] Americans with Disabilities Act
- [ ] Age Discrimination in Employment Act
- [ ] Pregnancy Act of 1978
- [ ] Equal Pay Act of 1963
- [ ] Genetic Information Non-discrimination Act (GINA)
- [ ] Vietnam Era Veteran's Readjustment Act (VEVRA)

NOTE: Do not forget to familiarize yourself with state and local employment laws.

EMPLOYEE AT WILL

In all states except Montana, there is a statute called Employment at will, which says that the employer or the employee can sever the relationship at any time for any reason with or without notice (as long as it is legal).

Using a Performance Improvement Plan (PIP)

DOCUMENTATION AND CONSISTENCY

Two important aspects of managing our employees are documentation and consistency. We need to document the employee's performance and actions throughout the employee life cycle. So if there is an instance where the company is audited or winds up in court, the employer has a detailed explanation through documentation of how the employee was treated. On the other hand, consistency is also important because if an employer is not consistent with how they treat their employees, they may inadvertently discriminate against an employee.

RESOURCES

Performance Improvement Plan Form
www.thebalancecareers.com/performance-improvement-plan-contents-and-sample-form-1918850

Stay Interview Checklist

PURPOSE

Stay Interviews are proactive practices that allow organizations and managers to learn what keeps employees. Rather than waiting until an employee puts in their notice and leaves, stay interviews help you gain insight into retaining employees while still employed. If done properly and with a goal of improvement, stay interviews can build trust, especially if meaningful changes are implemented based on the results. This *Ultimate HR Checklist* will help you make a stay interview process to create employees who are engaged in the mission and perform at high levels.

Stay Interview Checklist

- [ ] Schedule a one-hour meeting with them.
- [ ] Review proactive listening skills.
- [ ] Interview Employees.
- [ ] Ask questions about

    - *Positive Work Traits*—On your way to work each day, what parts of the day do you most look forward to?
    - *Retention*—What factors make you want to stay with the organization?
    - *Learning and Career Goals*—What opportunities are you taking advantage of to grow your skills?
    - *Flight Risks*—What causes you frustration daily?
    - *Support*—What support do you need to do your job well?
    - *Recognition*—What recognition do you like to receive?

- [ ] Compile the information into the trends you heard during the interview.

    - Why are people staying?
    - What would cause someone to leave?

- [ ] Decide what actions the organization can take to increase employee retention.
- [ ] Create an Action Plan start with the easy and build to the hard.
- [ ] Take Action.
- [ ] Repeat.

Stay Interview Checklist

LEGAL CONCERNS

Be consistent and fair with how stay interviews are done.

RESOURCES

Finnegan Institute
www.finneganinstitute.com/stay-interviews/

Training/Instructional Design Checklist

PURPOSE

Creating training for the workplace can be challenging yet rewarding. To help, a framework was created to provide professionals with a systematic and consistent process. The ADDIE model is a common and popular framework for designing instruction. ADDIE is an acronym representing the five stages of the instructional design process: Analysis, Design, Development, Implementation, and Evaluation.

DEFINITIONS

Training: Helping an employee be more effective at their job by teaching them a specific skill or knowledge set.

Training/Instructional Design Checklist

ANALYZE PHASE
- ☐ Define the problem
- ☐ Identify the source of the problem
- ☐ Determine possible solutions

DESIGN PHASE
- ☐ Use the outputs from the Analyze phase to plan a strategy for developing the instruction.
- ☐ Outline how to reach the instructional goals determined during the Analyze phase
- ☐ Expand the instructional foundation

DEVELOPMENT PHASE
- ☐ Build on both the Analyze and Design phases.
- ☐ Generate the lesson plans and lesson materials
- ☐ Develop the instruction and any supporting documentation/tools

IMPLEMENTATION PHASE
- ☐ Deliver the instruction

EVALUATION PHASE
- ☐ Measure the effectiveness and efficiency of the instruction

Training/Instructional Design Checklist

LEGAL CONCERNS

Be consistent and be fair, and don't forget to document the employees' time spent training.

RESOURCES

Association for Talent Development
www.td.org

Pryor Learning
www.pryor.com

Employee Retention Checklist

PURPOSE

One factor in a successful organization is the length of employee retention. The longer the length of the employee, the less reduction in institutional knowledge, reduction in turnover costs, and increased stability across the organization. This checklist provides a list of actions you can take to help retain employees across your organization.

NOTE

The Team at HR Stories recognizes that a 100 percent retention rate is not possible, nor is it beneficial to an organization. Turnover should be expected but controlled. The list we have created is an optimal list, and we realize that not every organization can do everything on this list, but by doing one or two, you will have better employee retention.

DEFINITIONS:

Employee retention is the percentage of employees who stay during any given time period.

Employee turnover is the percentage of employees who leave during any given time period.

Employee Tenure is the average length of time an employee stays with your company.

Employee Retention Checklists

CALCULATE YOUR EMPLOYEE TURNOVER RATE:

The # of employee separations / Average # of Employees) x 100

STEPS TO CALCULATING THE TURNOVER RATE:

1. Decide on the Reporting Period.
2. Calculate the Average # of Employees.
3. Note the Number of Separations.
4. Divide the # of Separations by the Avg. # of Employees.
5. Multiply by 100.

CALCULATE THE RETENTION RATE:

The # of employees at end / the # of employees at start) x 100

STEPS TO CALCULATE THE RETENTION RATE:

1. Decide on the Reporting Period
2. Calculate the # of Employees at the end of the reporting time period. (Don't include any new hires during this period.)
3. Calculate the # of employees at the beginning of the reporting time period.
4. Divide # of employees who remained by the number of employees who started
5. Multiply by 100

CALCULATE THE EMPLOYEE TENURE RATE:

Employee Tenure: *Sum of the length of tenure for all employees/# of employees*

STEPS TO CALCULATE THE EMPLOYEE TENURE:

1. Sum the length of tenure (number of years and months with the company) for all employees
2. Sum the # of all employees
3. Divide the Sum of the length of tenure by the # of employees.

Employee Retention Checklists

CALCULATE THE ENGAGEMENT COST (INTANGIBLE COSTS):

The cost of low morale, team performance, loss of institutional knowledge, and other more intangible items indirectly impact how profitable the business is.

USE SURVEYS AND INFORMAL MEETINGS TO CALCULATE THE ENGAGEMENT COSTS:

- [ ] Is organizational productivity remaining the same?
- [ ] Are they engaged in the mission of the organization?
- [ ] How do employees feel about the organization?
- [ ] How do they rate their morale?
- [ ] How are their stress levels?
- [ ] Are they feeling burned out?

CALCULATE THE FINANCIAL COST (TANGIBLE):

The amount of money it costs the company to hire a new employee and to get that employee up to the average productivity levels.

- [ ] The "I'm Leaving Soon" Costs
- [ ] Cost of Covering the Responsibilities
- [ ] Cost to Fill the Vacant Position Advertising
- [ ] Screening (Assessments, Background Checks, etc.)
- [ ] Selection
- [ ] Time of HR, Hiring Managers, and others involved in this process
- [ ] Onboarding & Orientation Costs Trainer Costs
- [ ] Hiring Manager Costs
- [ ] Productivity Ramp-up Costs: The 60-to-90-day period where the employee goes from learning to production.

HIRE FOR LONGEVITY:

When hiring employees, our main concentration is on the employee's ability to do the job; however, we should also focus on the employee's ability to do the job long-term.

ACTION STEPS YOU CAN TAKE...

- [ ] Write the Job Posting to ensure long-tenure employees apply.
- [ ] Discuss Organizational Mission
- [ ] Sell the Job and the Company
- [ ] Provide Details about the Job
- [ ] Don't over-promise
- [ ] Application Review Inspect Resumes for tenure at previous jobs
- [ ] Note the growth of the candidate
- [ ] Interview: Ask questions relating to tenure, such as...
  - Why are you leaving your current employer?
  - What makes a great work environment for you?
  - How do you build relationships at work?
- [ ] Ask Questions to determine fit with the company culture
- [ ] Determine short- and long-term goals.

STRENGTHEN ORIENTATION AND ONBOARDING

Orientation and onboarding are the processes of welcoming employees into the organization and providing them with any necessary information they will need to be successful in the company. We know those individuals who feel accepted and valued will stay longer with the company. This starts on day one.

- [ ] Making employees feel welcome
- [ ] Make sure their workplace is ready
- [ ] Greet them at the door
- [ ] Introduce them to coworkers
- [ ] Give them company SWAG
- [ ] Respect Them (viewpoint)
- [ ] Regular Check-ins
- [ ] Situational Knowledge Company Mission, Vision & Values
- [ ] Logistics
- [ ] Coworkers
- [ ] Acronyms (Formal and Informal)
- [ ] Employee Handbook

Note: One of the most important things leaders can do is clearly communicate to new employees exactly what is expected from their employees.

Employee Retention Checklists

BOOST PAY AND BENEFITS:

Thirty-seven percent of employees say that they would leave if their pay were too low. Understanding how much your employee expects to be paid is critical to longevity.

- [ ] Review compensation levels on a regular basis
- [ ] Review benefit levels on a regular basis
- [ ] Create consistent salary levels across your organization.
- [ ] Check the benefits you offer.
    - [ ] Health Insurance
    - [ ] Vision Insurance
    - [ ] Vacation Time
    - [ ] Personal Time Off
    - [ ] Paid Family Leave
    - [ ] Paternity Leave
    - [ ] Professional Development
    - [ ] Pet Insurance
    - [ ] Financial Wellness
    - [ ] Dental Insurance
    - [ ] Life Insurance
    - [ ] Sick Time
    - [ ] Retirement Plans
    - [ ] Maternity Leave
    - [ ] Mental Health Insurance
    - [ ] Disability Insurance
    - [ ] Tuition Assistance
    - [ ] Day Care Services

FLEXIBILITY IN THE WORKPLACE

80% of employees said they'd be more loyal to employers if they provided flexible work arrangements.

- [ ] *Location*: Does the employee have to work in a specific location or is there flexibility for them to choose their location?
- [ ] *Time*: How set our employee schedules? Can they be changed based on the employee's needs?
- [ ] *Culture*: Are the leaders modeling flexibility in their work?
- [ ] *Work Procedures:* Is there flexibility in how something is accomplished? Are new ideas encouraged?
- [ ] *Tasks*: Does the employee have control over their daily tasks?

Employee Retention Checklists

OPPORTUNITY FOR GROWTH

31% percent of employees indicated the primary reasons to quit are a lack of perceived progression and reskilling and upskilling opportunities at work. 68% percent of employees say they would stay with their employers throughout their career if the employer made an effort to upskill them.

- [ ] Create Career Path Statements for your employees.
- [ ] Start development from day one. Provide situational knowledge.
- [ ] Assess employee's strengths and opportunities.
- [ ] Provide the necessary training for them to excel in their role.
- [ ] Develop employee's strengths training.
- [ ] Mentorship
- [ ] Job Assignments
- [ ] Career Shadowing Programs

BUILD A STRONG WORKPLACE ENVIRONMENT

A recent study by Frontier in Public Health shows a direct correlation between the work environment and the performance levels of the employees and their commitment to the employer.

- [ ] Communicate and enforce anti-discrimination and harassment policies.
- [ ] Place an emphasis on Diversity, Equity, Inclusion and Belonging Efforts
- [ ] No tolerance policies for hate speech, violence, bullying and harassment
- [ ] Recognition programs
- [ ] Accept failure as part of the learning process
- [ ] Introduce wellness programs around physical, mental, family and financial health
- [ ] Have non-related work events
- [ ] Create a mentor program
- [ ] Treat Employees like customers.

Employee Retention Checklists

BUILD YOUR LEADERSHIP TEAM

In Jim Clifton and Jim Harter's book, It's the Manager, the Gallup organization's research shows that 70% of the variance in team engagement is determined solely by the manager. 57% of employees quit their jobs in 2021 because they felt disrespected. 62% of employees quit their job due to a toxic company culture.

In the employee's eyes their manager is the company.

LEADERSHIP SKILLS:

Leadership Skills	Empathic	Decisiveness
Organized	Commitment	Trustworthy
Time Management	High-Level Communication	Innovative
Confidence	Discipline	Knowledgeable
Honesty	Delegation	Effective Listening
Responsible	Respect	Energized/Passionate

Employee Retention Checklists

LEGAL CONCERNS

Ensure that the organization consistently follows all employment laws, in particular Title VII of the Civil Rights Act and other discrimination laws such as the ADEA, GINA, PWFA, Equal Pay Act, etc.

RESOURCES:

U.S. Bureau of Labor Statistics
www.bls.gov

John Thalheimer, *Stay Interviews* (True Star Leadership)

Jim Clifton and Jim Harter, *It's the Manager* (Gallup Press, 2019)

Forbes: Why Flexible Work Boosts Employee Productivity
www.forbes.com/sites/carolinecastrillon/2022/03/23/why-flexible-work-boosts-employee-productivity

Trinet: Trends and Insights
www.zenefits.com/workest/7-big-statistics-about-the-state-of-flexible-work-arrangements

Keeping the Organization Safe

Crisis Response Checklist

PURPOSE

Crisis situations happen, and in business, you need to be prepared. Crisis management is the process undertaken by any organization to prevent, prepare for, and respond to events that threaten to harm people or property, seriously interrupt operations, damage reputation, or impact the bottom line. HR professionals can help their companies by working with all stakeholders to follow the steps below to protect the company and employees.

DEFINITIONS

Crisis: A deviation from the normal operations of an organization that causes significant damage or concern.

Crisis Management: A process undertaken by any organization to prevent, prepare for and respond to events that threaten to harm people or property, seriously interrupt operations, damage reputation, or impact the bottom line.

Crisis Response Checklist

IN ADVANCE

- [ ] Discuss Possible Crisis Scenarios
    - Weather Event
    - Loss of Data
    - Power Outage
    - Disgruntled Employees
    - Critical Equipment Malfunction
    - Financial Crisis
    - Pandemic
    - Chain Supply Failure
    - Media Coverage
    - What else could it be for your business
- [ ] Conduct a Risk Analysis on the high probability events
- [ ] Decide on Initiation Procedure—what level initiates the Crisis Management Plan
- [ ] Assign an Emergency Response Coordinator
- [ ] Build a Crisis Response Team
- [ ] Assign Internal and External Spokesperson
- [ ] Determine Authority Levels for Crisis
- [ ] Develop communication protocol
- [ ] Create Response Plan
    - Brainstorm what-if scenarios
    - Don't forget your organization's Vision and Values
    - Detail steps to be taken and documented in simple steps
    - Assign people responsibilities and authorization levels for each step
    - Create an internal communication plan—who and how will the company communicate internally. Include contact information for all employees, supplies, vendors, etc.
    - Create an external communication plan—who and how will the company communicate externally. Include contact information for media outlets, etc.
    - Build prepared internal and external communication statements
    - Determine what resources will be necessary and how they will be quickly acquired
- [ ] Train Teams Involved
    - Practice scenarios
    - Table walkthroughs
    - Full-scale walkthroughs
- [ ] Update plans as necessary

Crisis Response Checklist

DURING A CRISIS

- [ ] Take a deep breath
- [ ] Determine the root cause of the crisis
- [ ] Assign Command to Emergency Coordinator
- [ ] Activate Emergency Protocol—communicate to leads, follow the plan as possible, communicate Deviations from the plan
- [ ] Communicate following actions to Stakeholders
- [ ] Focus on Employee Base
- [ ] Continue to follow the program—limit damage
- [ ] Increase communication to stakeholders
- [ ] Work to increase organizational value

AFTER CRISIS

- [ ] Do an After-Action Report
  - Note what went well
  - Note what went bad
  - Update plan based on findings
- [ ] Reward extraordinary effort
- [ ] Communication Findings and Next Actions

Crisis Response Checklist

LEGAL CONCERNS

Organizations must work within the confines of the laws and regulations of the crisis.

RESOURCES

U.S. Small Business Administration
www.sba.gov/funding-programs/disaster-assistance
www.sba.gov/business-guide/manage-your-business/prepare-emergencies

Employee Safety Program Checklist

PURPOSE

The main goal of safety and health programs is to prevent workplace injuries, illnesses, and deaths and the suffering and financial hardship these events can cause for workers, their families, and employers. The recommended practices use a proactive approach to managing workplace safety and health. Traditional approaches are often reactive —that is, problems are addressed only after a worker is injured or becomes sick, a new standard or regulation is published, or an outside inspection finds an issue that must be fixed. These recommended practices recognize that finding and fixing hazards before they cause injury or illness is a far more effective approach.

This Employee Safety Program *Ultimate HR Checklist* is adopted from OSHA.gov—Recommended Practices for Safety and Health Programs.

DEFINITIONS

OSHA General Clause: Each employer shall furnish their employee's employment and a place of employment free from recognized hazards that are causing or are likely to cause death or serious physical harm to their employees. (2) Each employer share comply with occupational safety and health standards promulgated under this act. (3) Each employee shall comply with occupational safety and health standards and all rules, regulations, and orders issued under this Act that are applicable to his actions and conduct.

Employer: Any person engaged in commerce or in an industry or activity affecting commerce who employs 50 or more employees for each working day during each of 20 or more calendar workweeks in the current or preceding calendar year.

Employee: Any individual employed by an employer.

Employee Safety Program Checklist

ACTION ITEM 1:

ENCOURAGE WORKERS TO PARTICIPATE IN THE PROGRAM

- [ ] Give workers the necessary time and resources to participate in the program
- [ ] Acknowledge and provide positive reinforcement to those who participate in the program
- [ ] Create and maintain an open-door policy that invites workers to talk to managers about safety and health and to make suggestions

ACTION ITEM 2:

ENCOURAGE WORKERS TO REPORT SAFETY AND HEALTH CONCERNS

- [ ] Establish a process for workers to report injuries, illnesses, close calls/near misses, hazards, and other safety and health concerns, and respond to reports promptly. Include an option for anonymous reporting to reduce fear of reprisal.1
- [ ] Report back to workers routinely and frequently about action taken in response to their concerns and suggestions.
- [ ] Emphasize that management will use reported information only to improve workplace safety and health and that no worker will experience retaliation for bringing such information to management's attention (see Action Item 5).
- [ ] Empower all workers to initiate or request a temporary suspension or shut down any work activity or operation they believe unsafe.
- [ ] Involve workers in finding solutions to reported issues.

Employee Safety Program Checklist

ACTION ITEM 3:

GIVE WORKERS ACCESS TO SAFETY AND HEALTH INFORMATION

- [ ] Give workers the information they need to understand safety and health hazards and control measures in the workplace. Some OSHA standards require employers to make specific types of information available to workers, such as:
  - Safety Data Sheets (SDS)
  - Injury and illness data (may need to be redacted and aggregated to eliminate personal identifiers)
  - Results of environmental exposure monitoring conducted in the workplace (prevent disclosure of sensitive and personal information as required)
- [ ] Other helpful information for workers to review can include:
  - Chemical and equipment manufacturer safety recommendations
  - Workplace inspection reports
  - Incident investigation reports (prevent disclosure of sensitive and personal information as required)
  - Workplace job hazard analyses

ACTION ITEM 4:

INVOLVE WORKERS IN ALL ASPECTS OF THE PROGRAM

- [ ] Provide opportunities for workers to participate in all aspects of the program, including, but not limited to helping:
  - Develop the program and set goals.
  - Report hazards and develop solutions that improve safety and health.
  - Analyze hazards in each step of routine and non-routine jobs, tasks, and processes.
  - Define and document safe work practices.
  - Conduct site inspections.
  - Develop and revise safety procedures.
  - Participate in incident and close call/near-miss investigations.
  - Train current coworkers and new hires.
  - Develop, implement, and evaluate training programs.
  - Evaluate program performance and identify ways to improve it.
  - Take part in exposure monitoring and medical surveillance associated with health hazards.

ACTION ITEM 5:

REMOVE BARRIERS TO PARTICIPATION

- [ ] Ensure that workers from all levels of the organization can participate regardless of their skill level, education, or language.
- [ ] Provide frequent and regular feedback to show employees that their safety and health concerns are being heard and addressed.
- [ ] Authorize sufficient time and resources to facilitate worker participation; for example, hold safety and health meetings during regular working hours.
- [ ] Ensure that the program protects workers from being retaliated against for
- [ ] Reporting injuries, illnesses, and hazards
  - Participating in the program
  - Exercising their safety and health rights
- [ ] Ensure that other policies and programs do not discourage worker participation.
- [ ] Post the 11(c) Fact Sheet (found at www.whistleblowers.gov) in the workplace or otherwise make it available for easy access by workers.

Employee Safety Program Checklist

LEGAL CONCERNS

OCCUPATIONAL SAFETY AND HEALTH

According to the general clause of OSHA, employers are required to have a workplace free from recognized hazards that may cause death or serious harm. It is unethical to disregard or blatantly ignore the safety of our team members.

RESOURCES

Occupational Safety and Health Administration
- www.osha.gov/
- www.osha.gov/safety-management

U.S. Department of Labor – Workplace Safety and Health
- www.dol.gov/general/topic/safety-health

Merger/Acquisition Due Diligence Checklist

PURPOSE

HR professionals play pivotal roles in a merger or acquisition's core due diligence activity. Owners and Senior Management will expect the Human Resources function to participate and provide information to protect the company and discover any issues. During the Due Diligence phase, HR should be prepared to review the following items in this Checklist.

DEFINITIONS

Merger: Bringing together two organizations to operate as one.

Acquisition: Purchasing another organization and operating it as one.

Due Diligence: The reasonable steps taken to ensure when we acquire or merge with another organization to avoid harm to other persons, their property, or our organization.

Merger/Acquisition Due To Diligence Checklist

HR DOCUMENTS

- [ ] Names and locations of employees (complete employee census)
- [ ] I-9 forms
- [ ] Visa documents
- [ ] Benefit plans
- [ ] Performance review process

COMPENSATION DOCUMENTS

- [ ] Payroll documents
- [ ] Details of other non-monetary compensation
- [ ] Hourly wages rates by the job
- [ ] Salary schedules
- [ ] Number of employees in each position

POLICIES AND PROCEDURES

- [ ] The policy manual
- [ ] Employee handbook
- [ ] Supervisor/manager handbook

EQUAL OPPORTUNITY COMPLIANCE

- [ ] EEO-1 reports
- [ ] Affirmative action plans
- [ ] Government notices of compliance activity
- [ ] Consent decrees

LEGAL COMPLIANCE

- ☐ COBRA notices
- ☐ Active FMLA leave
- ☐ WARN compliance
- ☐ OSHA compliance
- ☐ Other Leave related policies and situations
- ☐ ERISA compliance

AGREEMENTS AND CONTRACTS

- ☐ Offer letters/employment contracts
- ☐ Collective bargaining agreement
- ☐ Ongoing negotiations
- ☐ Union activity
- ☐ Non-compete contracts
- ☐ Confidentiality agreements
- ☐ Retirement and pensions
- ☐ Any other employee contracts that could preempt at-will
- ☐ Golden contracts in place (handcuffs, parachute, life jacket)

LEGAL EXPOSURE

- ☐ Pending or resolved sexual harassment claims
- ☐ Termination disputes
- ☐ Violations of state/federal law
- ☐ Active worker's compensation claims
- ☐ Unpaid wages and claims
- ☐ Other litigation situations

OTHER ITEMS

- ☐ Review and audit of HRIS/HRM system
- ☐ Contact all HR related vendors, carriers, suppliers
- ☐ Media relations
- ☐ Grievance history
- ☐ Communication plan and timeline
- ☐ Passwords accounted for

Merger/Acquisition Due To Diligence Checklist

TAKE-OVER DAY CONSIDERATIONS

- [ ] Date and time merger/acquisition is officially and legally closed on
- [ ] Transition team in place and located in key areas on closing/take-over day
- [ ] Assets of the new entity, including any cash banks and equipment, are secured
- [ ] All-employee meeting scheduled with agenda
- [ ] Benefits and paperwork ready for new employee
- [ ] List of FAQs–frequently asked questions
- [ ] ID's and name badges

STANDARD HR DUE TO DILIGENCE CHECKLIST

- [ ] National political, social, and cultural framework
- [ ] Strategy, workforce composition, and organization
- [ ] HR administration and measurement
- [ ] Legal framework
- [ ] Recruitment
- [ ] Review of critical contracts of employment
- [ ] Training and development
- [ ] Remuneration and pay administration
- [ ] Benefits
- [ ] Sick leave and sick pay and benefits
- [ ] Employee financial participation
- [ ] Performance and quality management
- [ ] Working time
- [ ] Leave and time-off
- [ ] Equality
- [ ] Employee representation and corporate communication
- [ ] Security and safety
- [ ] Internal rules, discipline, and grievance procedures
- [ ] Termination of contract
- [ ] Retirement and pensions

Merger/Acquisition Due To Diligence Checklist

LEGAL CONCERNS

Every aspect of the merger or acquisition will have legal concerns from proper I-9s, employee performance documentation, recruitment, safety, and health, etc.

RESOURCES

Martin Goodman and Pete Burgess, *IDS International HR Due Diligence Checklist* (Incomes Data Services, 2005)

> The Human Aspect of M&A Integration
> dealroom.net/blog/the-human-aspect-of-m-a-integration

Hazards Assessment Identification Checklist

PURPOSE

An assessment of risk helps employers understand hazards in the context of their workplace and prioritize hazards for permanent control. If you have one or more employees, you must do a Hazard Assessment. If you have ten or more employees, that assessment must be in writing.

This Hazard Identification and Assessment Checklist is adopted from OSHA.gov—Recommended Practices for Safety and Health Programs.

DEFINITIONS

OSHA General Clause: Each employer shall furnish to their employee's employment and a place of employment that are free from recognized hazards that are causing or are likely to cause death or serious physical harm to their employees. (2) Each employer share comply with occupational safety and health standards promulgated under this act. (3) Each employee shall comply with occupational safety and health standards and all rules, regulations, and orders issued under this Act that is applicable to his actions and conduct.

Employer: Any person engaged in commerce or in an industry or activity affecting commerce who employs 50 or more employees for each working day during each of 20 or more calendar workweeks in the current or preceding calendar year.

Employee: Any individual employed by an employer.

Hazards Assessment Identification Checklist

ACTION ITEM 1:

COLLECT EXISTING INFORMATION ABOUT WORKPLACE HAZARDS

- [ ] Equipment and machinery operating manuals.
- [ ] Safety Data Sheets (SDS) provided by chemical manufacturers.
- [ ] Self-inspection reports and inspection reports from insurance carriers, government agencies, and consultants.
- [ ] Records of previous injuries and illnesses, such as OSHA 300 and 301 logs and reports of incident investigations.
- [ ] Workers' compensation records and reports.
- [ ] Patterns of frequently occurring injuries and illnesses.
- [ ] Exposure monitoring results, industrial hygiene assessments, and medical records (appropriately redacted to ensure patient/worker privacy).
- [ ] Existing safety and health programs (lockout/tag out, confined spaces, process safety management, personal protective equipment, etc.).
- [ ] Input from workers, including surveys or minutes from safety and health committee meetings.
- [ ] Results of job hazard analyses, also known as job safety analyses.

ACTION ITEM 2:

INSPECT THE WORKPLACE FOR SAFETY HAZARD

- [ ] Conduct regular inspections of all operations, equipment, work areas, and facilities. Have workers participate on the inspection team and talk to them about hazards that they see or report.
- [ ] Be sure to document inspections so you can later verify that hazardous conditions are corrected. Take photos or videos of problem areas to facilitate later discussion and brainstorming about how to control them and use them as learning aids.
- [ ] Include all areas and activities in these inspections, such as storage and warehousing, facility, and equipment maintenance, purchasing, and office functions, and the actions of on-site contractors, subcontractors, and temporary employees.
- [ ] Regularly inspect both plant vehicles (e.g., forklifts, powered industrial trucks) and transportation vehicles (e.g., cars, trucks).

Hazards Assessment Identification Checklist

- [ ] Use checklists that highlight things to look for. Typical hazards fall into several major categories, such as those listed below; each workplace will have its own list:
  - General housekeeping
  - Slip, trip, and fall hazards
  - Electrical hazards
  - Equipment operation
  - Equipment maintenance
  - Fire protection
  - Work organization and process flow (including staffing and scheduling)
  - Work practices
  - Workplace violence
  - Ergonomic problems
  - Lack of emergency procedures
- [ ] Before changing operations, workstations, or workflow; making significant organizational changes, or introducing new equipment, materials, or processes, seek the input of workers and evaluate the planned changes for potential hazards and related risks.

ACTION ITEM 3:

IDENTIFY HEALTH HAZARDS

- [ ] Identify *chemical hazards* – review SDS and product labels to identify chemicals in your workplace that have low exposure limits, are highly volatile or are used in large quantities or in unventilated spaces. Identify activities that may result in skin exposure to chemicals.
- [ ] Identify *physical hazards* –identify any exposures to excessive noise (areas where you must raise your voice to be heard by others), elevated heat (indoor and outdoor), or sources of radiation (radioactive materials, X-rays, or radio frequency radiation).
- [ ] Identify *biological hazards* –determine whether workers may be exposed to sources of infectious diseases, molds, toxic or poisonous plants, or animal materials (fur or scat) capable of causing allergic reactions or occupational asthma.
- [ ] Identify *ergonomic risk factors* –examine work activities requiring heavy lifting, above shoulder height, repetitive motions, or tasks with significant vibration.
- [ ] Conduct *quantitative exposure assessments* –when possible, using air sampling or direct-reading instruments.
- [ ] *Review medical records* –to identify cases of musculoskeletal injuries, skin irritation or dermatitis, hearing loss, or lung disease that may be related to workplace exposures.

ACTION ITEM 4:

CONDUCT INCIDENT INVESTIGATIONS

- [ ] Develop a clear plan and procedure for conducting incident investigations so that an investigation can begin immediately when an incident occurs. The plan should cover items such as:
- [ ] Who will be involved?
  - Lines of communication
  - Materials, equipment, and supplies needed
  - Reporting forms and templates
- [ ] Train investigative teams on incident investigation techniques, emphasizing objectivity and open-mindedness throughout the investigation process.
- [ ] Conduct investigations with a trained team that includes management and workers representatives.
- [ ] Investigate close calls/near misses.
- [ ] Identify and analyze root causes to address underlying program shortcomings that allowed the incidents to happen.
- [ ] Communicate the investigation results to managers, supervisors, and workers to prevent a recurrence.

ACTION ITEM 5:

IDENTIFY HAZARDS ASSOCIATED WITH EMERGENCY AND NON-ROUTINE SITUATIONS

- [ ] Identify foreseeable emergency scenarios and non-routine tasks, considering the types of material and equipment in use and the location within the facility. Scenarios such as the following may be foreseeable:
  - Fires and explosions
  - Chemical releases
  - Hazardous material spills
  - Startups after planned or unplanned equipment shutdowns
  - Non-routine tasks, such as infrequently performed maintenance activities
  - Structural collapse
  - Disease outbreaks
  - Weather emergencies and natural disasters
  - Medical emergencies
  - Workplace violence

Hazards Assessment Identification Checklist

ACTION ITEM 6:

CHARACTERIZE THE NATURE OF IDENTIFIED HAZARDS, IDENTIFY INTERIM CONTROL MEASURES, AND PRIORITIZE THE HAZARDS FOR CONTROL

- [ ] Evaluate each hazard by considering the severity of potential outcomes, the likelihood that an event or exposure will occur, and the number of workers who might be exposed.
- [ ] Use interim control measures to protect workers until more permanent solutions can be implemented.
- [ ] Prioritize the hazards so that those presenting the greatest risk are addressed first. Note, however, that employers have an ongoing obligation to control all serious recognized hazards and to protect workers.

Hazards Assessment Identification Checklist

LEGAL CONCERNS

OSHA GENERAL CLAUSE

Each employer shall furnish to their employee's employment and a place of employment that are free from recognized hazards that are causing or are likely to cause death or serious physical harm to their employees. (2) Each employer share comply with occupational safety and health standards promulgated under this act. (3) Each employee shall comply with occupational safety and health standards and all rules, regulations, and orders issued under this Act that is applicable to his actions and conduct.

RESOURCES

Occupational Safety and Health Administration
www.osha.gov/
www.osha.gov/safety-management

U.S. Department of Labor– Workplace Safety and Health
www.dol.gov/general/topic/safety-health

OSHA Inspection Prep Checklist

PURPOSE

OSHA Compliance Officer/Inspector visits are often unannounced. Make sure the following items are in order and easily accessible so that you can show due diligence and reasonable faith effort with complying with all OSHA Standards, Programs, and Guidelines. Review the OSHA Inspection Visit Checklist for more information on what to do when the Inspector visits.

DEFINITIONS

OSHA General Clause: Each employer shall furnish to their employee's employment and a place of employment that are free from recognized hazards that are causing or are likely to cause death or serious physical harm to their employees. (2) Each employer share comply with occupational safety and health standards promulgated under this act. (3) Each employee shall comply with occupational safety and health standards and all rules, regulations, and orders issued under this Act that are applicable to his actions and conduct.

Employer: Any person engaged in commerce or in an industry or activity affecting commerce who employs 50 or more employees for each working day during each of 20 or more calendar workweeks in the current or preceding calendar year.

Employee: Any individual employed by an employer.

OSHA Inspection Prep Checklist

- [ ] Employee training records (this is probably the FIRST thing OSHA will ask for)
- [ ] OSHA poster is in place
- [ ] At a minimum, have the following current and prior three years ready to show:
  - OSHA 300 logs
  - HazCom Program
  - SDS records
  - Confined space programs
  - Lockout/Tagout
  - Respiratory protection program
  - Bloodborne Pathogens
  - Emergency Evacuation procedures
  - Personal Protective Equipment (PPE) program
  - Self-inspection reports
  - Safety Committee meeting notes
  - Forms of any previously identified and corrected hazards
  - Any other work hazards program or documents specific to your industry
  - Relevant records are required to be kept by under the OSHA Act and OSHA standards or regulations
- [ ] Train your staff (usually Reception area, Security, front-line operations management) to be on the lookout for OSHA inspection activity
- [ ] Train staff on procedures when they observe or encounter an OSHA Inspector
  - Being polite, professional, cooperative, and responsive
  - Not to volunteer or over-share information
  - Where the Inspector will wait and conduct any interviews
  - What to expect in the inspection process
- [ ] Sometimes OSHA sends a letter or makes a phone call—train staff on the procedures for handling these situations
- [ ] Be familiar with OSHA credentials so you can verify them upon arrival
- [ ] Decide your company practice on if you will allow the Inspector to enter the property upon arrival or if you will require them to have a search warrant
- [ ] Create and maintain a list of relevant management that need to be summoned in the event of an OSHA inspection
- [ ] Have a front-line employee representative identified—usually a member of your Safety Committee of if organized, the Union Steward or Safety Rep.
- [ ] Identify your Trade Secrets to verify them with the Inspector as they are obligated to protect that confidentiality.

OSHA Inspection Prep Checklist

- [ ] Have a kit ready with the following items:
    - Notebook and pen
    - Camera or video camera
    - Measuring tape
    - Flashlight
- [ ] Identify who will take notes of the inspection activity and observations
- [ ] Identify who will take pictures and video of the inspection activity and observations
- [ ] Know and understand the OSHA General Duty Clause and how it applies to your business facilities, job sites, and employee job functions
- [ ] Collect employee feedback on potential hazards in the workplace
- [ ] Conduct monthly inspections of all work areas, equipment, vehicles, and facilities
- [ ] Fix and document all safety and health hazards as soon as possible
- [ ] Consider using the OSHA On-site Consultation Program

OSHA Inspection Prep Checklist

LEGAL CONCERNS

OSHA GENERAL CLAUSE

Each employer shall furnish to their employee's employment and a place of employment that are free from recognized hazards that are causing or are likely to cause death or serious physical harm to their employees. (2) Each employer share comply with occupational safety and health standards promulgated under this act. (3) Each employee shall comply with occupational safety and health standards and all rules, regulations, and orders issued under this Act that are applicable to his actions and conduct.

RESOURCES

Occupational Safety and Health Administration
www.osha.gov/
www.osha.gov/safety-management

U.S. Department of Labor— Workplace Safety and Health
www.dol.gov/general/topic/safety-health

OSHA Onsite Visit Inspection Checklist

PURPOSE

At some point in time, you may receive an unannounced visit from an OSHA Inspector. You need to pre-plan what to do when they show up at your workplace.

DEFINITIONS

OSHA General Clause: Each employer shall furnish to their employee's employment and a place of employment which are free from recognized hazards that are causing or are likely to cause death or serious physical harm to their employees. (2) Each employer share comply with occupational safety and health standards promulgated under this act. (3) Each employee shall comply with occupational safety and health standards and all rules, regulations, and orders issued under this Act that are applicable to his actions and conduct.

Employer: Any person engaged in commerce or in an industry or activity affecting commerce who employs 50 or more employees for each working day during each of 20 or more calendar workweeks in the current or preceding calendar year.

Employee: Any individual employed by an employer.

OSHA Onsite Visit Inspection Checklist

IF YOU RECEIVE A PHONE CALL OR LETTER

- [ ] You must respond within ten days
- [ ] Provide a thorough response showing compliance or correction—use photographs, receipts of purchase for safety equipment, proof of training

IF YOU RECEIVE A VISIT FROM AN OSHA INSPECTOR (COMPLIANCE OFFICER)

- [ ] Do not panic—OSHA inspections are almost always unannounced
- [ ] Be polite when you greet the Inspector (also known as a Compliance Officer)
- [ ] OSHA Inspectors will show you their credentials and state the reason for their visit—according to OSHA Field Manual, this is the "opening conference."
- [ ] Verify and note any "trade secrets" to the OSHA Inspector
- [ ] You may restrict admittance until appropriate management is on-site
- [ ] While it is not advisable, you may require the OSHA Inspector to have a search warrant before any inspection
- [ ] Determine the reason for the inspection (OSHA has five reasons)
  - Employee complaint
  - Fatality/Amputation/Serious Injury
  - Focus on your Industry
  - Media-based—report of a situation like a fire or explosion
  - Random inspection
- [ ] Obtain a copy of the complaint from the Inspector
- [ ] Do not speculate who made the complaint
- [ ] Warn your managers to not speculate and thus attempt retaliation action
- [ ] Inspector may ask for an employee representative chosen by you (the employer)
- [ ] Define the areas the Inspector will need to see

- [ ] Do not offer a property or plant tour of the facility
- [ ] Escort the Inspector to the targeted areas via a low controversial route (one in which they are least likely to notice safety violations)
- [ ] Always stay with the Inspector but DO NOT volunteer any information

OSHA Onsite Visit Inspection Checklist

- [ ] Only provide relevant records upon request. Offer to send them via mail after inspection
- [ ] Take notes of the route you walk, the things that they observe and appear to observe. Write down the times they visited certain areas and the length of time that they stayed in each area
- [ ] OSHA Inspectors like to take photographs. You should be prepared to photograph the same items that they do (including video if applicable)
- [ ] OSHA Inspector may privately interview members of management—company representatives may sit in on those interviews
- [ ] OSHA Inspector may privately interview hourly employees—company representatives may NOT sit in on those interviews
- [ ] The OSHA Inspector will have a final meeting with company management before they leave—this is called the "Closing Conference."
- [ ] Allow the Inspector to address their findings. Take careful notes on their statements at the Closing Conference
- [ ] If you are less than completely clear about their findings, restate your understanding of their findings to the Inspector for agreement
- [ ] Be sure to ask for answers.
- [ ] What are the alleged violations?
- [ ] What are the CSHO's next steps in the process?
- [ ] Will there be a further on-site inspection before issuing any citations or a 'decision not to issue'?
- [ ] When can your company expect to receive any 'decision not to issue' or quotations?
- [ ] Create an OSHA inspection file—all photos and notes. Copies of reports and records given to OSHA should all be in the file.
- [ ] Fix minor violations immediately to show "good faith" and be prepared to have a timeline for any other alleged violations
- [ ] Take photos of the corrections
- [ ] If your company is cited with violations, you may also appeal to the Area Director within 15 working days

OSHA Onsite Visit Inspection Checklist

LEGAL CONCERNS

OSHA GENERAL CLAUSE

Each employer shall furnish to their employee's employment and a place of employment that are free from recognized hazards that are causing or are likely to cause death or serious physical harm to their employees. (2) Each employer share comply with occupational safety and health standards promulgated under this act. (3) Each employee shall comply with occupational safety and health standards and all rules, regulations, and orders issued under this Act that are applicable to his actions and conduct.

RESOURCES

Occupational Safety and Health Administration
www.osha.gov/
www.osha.gov/safety-management

U.S. Department of Labor— Workplace Safety and Health
www.dol.gov/general/topic/safety-health

Threat Assessment Checklist

PURPOSE

Threats towards the company, employees, information technology, or property should be considered serious until deemed otherwise. This checklist will provide steps to help you assess the issue and provide the necessary next actions. If you feel the threat is serious, call the police or appropriate authority immediately.

DEFINITIONS

Threat: An expression of intention to inflict injury or damage to your organization. A threat could be one of violence against an employee or property. It can also be a general threat against the organization and its customers.

Threat Assessment Checklist

BEFORE A THREAT HAPPENS

- [ ] Create and communicate a firm anti-violence policy
- [ ] Do employee background checks
- [ ] Develop a threat assessment form
- [ ] Review IT Safety Protocol
- [ ] Review building safety protocol
- [ ] Ask the police or hire an agency to come and do a "targeting hardening" assessment
- [ ] Practice safety drills
- [ ] Train employees in proper safety protocol in case of an emergency or active shooter
- [ ] Create and communicate communication plan in case of a threat
- [ ] HR and Executive team discuss indicators of violent tendencies

WHEN A THREAT HAPPENS

- [ ] Capture the following information.
  - Who or what was threatened?
  - How did you learn about the threat?
  - Are there any recordings of the threat?
  - When did you learn about the threat?
  - Who made the threat? Where did the threat originate?
- [ ] Describe the threat. The language used actions, gestures, etc.
- [ ] Review personnel file of employee or ex-employee involved for previous issues
- [ ] If necessary, call the police or other authority
- [ ] Account for all employees on the property
- [ ] Lockdown buildings
- [ ] Ask Employees to shelter in place, if necessary
- [ ] Lockdown systems
- [ ] Notify impacted employees of the incident
  - What happened (generalities)
  - What is known and unknown
  - What you want them to do
  - What they should not do
  - When you will issue the next communication

Threat Assessment Checklist

- [ ] If an employee or terminated employee, call an employment lawyer and review legal concerns
- [ ] Focus on people safety first, then systems, and then the property
- [ ] Have a spokesperson ready to discuss the incident

AFTER A THREAT INCIDENT

- [ ] Check on employees—hire a counselor to talk to employees
- [ ] Check on systems—hire an outside expert to review systems
- [ ] Check on buildings—do a manual check of all property
- [ ] Capture and save necessary documentation
- [ ] Work with the appropriate authorities to reduce risk
- [ ] Work with your employment lawyer to reduce liability
- [ ] In guidance with an attorney, send out a press release
- [ ] Do an after-action report. What went well? What did not go well, and what will you change in the future?
- [ ] Return to business as soon as possible

Threat Assessment Checklist

LEGAL CONCERNS

OSHA GENERAL CLAUSE

Each employer shall furnish to their employee's employment and a place of employment that are free from recognized hazards that are causing or are likely to cause death or serious physical harm to their employees. (2) Each employer share comply with occupational safety and health standards promulgated under this act. (3) Each employee shall comply with occupational safety and health standards and all rules, regulations, and orders issued under this Act that are applicable to his actions and conduct.

Threats can be illegal, depending on the level of the threat. It is important to work with local, state, and federal agencies to help evaluate and eliminate the threat.

RESOURCES

Occupational Safety and Health Administration
www.osha.gov/workplace-violence

Workplace Violence Assessment Checklist

PURPOSE

This checklist helps identify present or potential workplace violence problems. Employers also may be aware of other serious hazards not listed here.

Designated competent and responsible observers can readily make periodic inspections to identify and evaluate workplace security hazards and threats of workplace violence. These inspections should be scheduled regularly when new, previously unidentified security hazards are recognized, when occupational deaths, injuries, or threats of damage occur, when a safety, health, and security program is established, and whenever workplace security conditions warrant an inspection.

Periodic inspections for security hazards include identifying and evaluating potential workplace security hazards and changes in employee work practices which may lead to compromising security.

DEFINITIONS

Threat: An expression of intention to inflict injury or damage to your organization. A threat could be one of violence against an employee or property. It can also be a general threat against the organization and its customers.

OSHA General Clause: Each employer shall furnish to their employee's employment and a place of employment that are free from recognized hazards that are causing or are likely to cause death or serious physical harm to their employees. (2) Each employer share comply with occupational safety and health standards promulgated under this act. (3) Each employee shall comply with occupational safety and health standards and all rules, regulations, and orders issued under this Act that are applicable to his own actions and conduct.

Employer: Any person engaged in commerce or in an industry or activity affecting commerce who employs 50 or more employees for each working day during each of 20 or more calendar workweeks in the current or preceding calendar year.

Employee: Any individual employed by an employer.

Workplace Violence Assessment Checklist

Please use the following checklist to identify and evaluate workplace security hazards. **TRUE** notations indicate a potential risk for serious security hazards:

T	F	
		This industry frequently confronts violent behavior and assaults of staff.
		Violence has occurred on the premises or in conducting business.
		Customers, clients, or coworkers assault, threaten, yell, push, or verbally abuse employees or use racial or sexual remarks.
		Employees are **NOT** required to report incidents or threats of violence to the employer regardless of injury or severity.
		Employees have **NOT** been trained by the employer to recognize and handle threatening, aggressive, or violent behavior.
		Violence is accepted as "part of the job" by some managers, supervisors, and/or employees.
		Access and freedom of movement within the workplace are **NOT** restricted to those persons who have a legitimate reason for being there.
		The workplace security system is inadequate-i.e., door locks malfunction, windows are not secure, and there are no physical barriers or containment systems.
		Employees or staff members have been assaulted, threatened, or verbally abused by clients and patients.
		Medical and counseling services have **NOT** been offered to employees who have been assaulted.
		Alarm systems such as panic alarm buttons, silent alarms, or personal electronic alarm systems are **NOT** being used for prompt security assistance.
		There is no regular training provided on the correct response to the alarm sounding.
		Alarm systems are **NOT** tested every month to assure correct function.
		Security guards are **NOT** employed at the workplace.
		Closed-circuit cameras and mirrors are **NOT** used to monitor dangerous areas.
		Metal detectors are **NOT** available or **NOT** used in the facility.
		Employees have **NOT** been trained to recognize and control hostile and escalating aggressive behaviors and to manage assaultive behavior.
		Employees **CAN NOT** adjust work schedules to use the "Buddy system" for visits to clients in areas where they feel threatened.
		Cellular phones or other communication devices are **NOT** made available to field staff to enable them to request aid.
		Vehicles are **NOT** maintained on a regular basis to ensure reliability and safety.
		Employees work where assistance is **NOT** quickly available.

Number of T (**TRUE**) notations: _____

All **TRUE** notations indicate a potential risk for serious security hazards and should be followed up with an investigation and formal documented assessment.

Workplace Violence Assessment Checklist

LEGAL CONCERNS

OSHA GENERAL CLAUSE

Each employer shall furnish to their employee's employment and a place of employment that are free from recognized hazards that are causing or are likely to cause death or serious physical harm to their employees. (2) Each employer share comply with occupational safety and health standards promulgated under this act. (3) Each employee shall comply with occupational safety and health standards and all rules, regulations, and orders issued under this Act that are applicable to his own actions and conduct.

Threats can be illegal, depending on the level of the threat. It is important to work with local, state, and federal agencies to help evaluate and eliminate the threat.

RESOURCES

Society for Human Resource Management

www.shrm.org/resourcesandtools/tools-and-samples/toolkits/pages/workplace-violence-prevention-and-response.aspx (membership site)

Occupational Safety and Health Administration

www.osha.gov/workplace-violence

Reducing Organizational Risk (Self Audits)

EEOC Notification Response Checklist

PURPOSE

The U.S. Equal Employment Opportunity Commission enforces federal laws prohibiting employment discrimination. These laws protect employees and job applicants against discrimination. If an employee or job applicant believes that they have been discriminated against at work, they can file a "Charge of Discrimination." When a charge is filed, it can be very upsetting to the employer. The EEOC Notification Response *Ultimate HR Checklist* will guide you through the process of how to respond when a charge is filed against your company. Remember, just because the EEOC is involved doesn't mean that the charge is valid, but you need to be prepared.

(See Legal Concerns below for a complete list of federal laws)

DEFINITIONS

Charge of Discrimination: A charge of discrimination is a signed statement asserting that an employer, union, or labor organization engaged in employment discrimination. It requests EEOC to take remedial action.

EPLI Carrier: Employment Practices Liability Insurance (EPLI) includes coverage for defense costs and damages related to various employment-related claims, including allegations of Wrongful Termination, Discrimination, Workplace Harassment, and Retaliation.

Retaliation: Retaliation is the most frequently alleged basis of discrimination in the federal sector and the most common discrimination finding in federal sector cases. The EEO laws prohibit punishing job applicants or employees for asserting their rights to be free from employment discrimination, including harassment. Asserting these EEO rights is called "protected activity," which can take many forms.

EEOC Notification Response Checklist

- [ ] Take the letter seriously—you usually only have 30 days to respond!
- [ ] Maintain composure and be professional
- [ ] Review the charge notice carefully—recognize that this is a "charge" or "complaint." It is NOT a determination of discrimination
- [ ] Notify your EPLI policy carrier
- [ ] Follow the directions on the EEOC charge notice
- [ ] Gather your information/Conduct a factual investigation
- [ ] Maintain notification of the charge on a need-to-know basis
- [ ] Do NOT confront the employee who made the complaint
- [ ] Ensure that the employee's manager DOES NOT confront the employee and cause a retaliation claim
- [ ] Inform the manager that they are to preserve ALL documentation and they are not to destroy or discard anything
- [ ] Provide your written response and any other requested information per the EEOC letter
- [ ] Respond to any additional EEOC requests—even if you believe they are frivolous and the charge is without merit
- [ ] Be responsive to a request to meet with the EEOC investigator
- [ ] If you have questions or require more time, contact the noted EEOC Investigator directly
- [ ] Consider the mediation process
- [ ] Contact legal counsel if appropriate
- [ ] Cooperation is key to showing a good faith effort with the EEOC Investigator and process.
- [ ] Do not be belligerent or rude to the EEOC Investigator...it will not advance your interests.

EEOC Notification Response Checklist

LEGAL CONCERNS

TITLE VII OF THE CIVIL RIGHTS ACT OF 1964

This law makes it illegal to discriminate against someone on the basis of race, color, religion, national origin, or sex. The law also makes it illegal to retaliate against a person because the person complained about discrimination, filed a charge of discrimination, or participated in an employment discrimination investigation or lawsuit. The law also requires that employers reasonably accommodate applicants' and employees' sincerely held religious practices, unless doing so would impose an undue hardship on the operation of the employer's business.

THE PREGNANCY DISCRIMINATION ACT

This law amended Title VII to make it illegal to discriminate against a woman because of pregnancy, childbirth, or a medical condition related to pregnancy or childbirth. The law also makes it illegal to retaliate against a person because the person complained about discrimination, filed a charge of discrimination, or participated in an employment discrimination investigation or lawsuit.

THE EQUAL PAY ACT OF 1963 (EPA)

This law makes it illegal to pay different wages to men and women if they perform equal work in the same workplace. The law also makes it illegal to retaliate against a person because the person complained about discrimination, filed a charge of discrimination, or participated in an employment discrimination investigation or lawsuit.

THE AGE DISCRIMINATION IN EMPLOYMENT ACT OF 1967 (ADEA)

This law protects people who are 40 or older from discrimination because of age. The law also makes it illegal to retaliate against a person because the person complained about discrimination, filed a charge of discrimination, or participated in an employment discrimination investigation or lawsuit.

TITLE I OF THE AMERICANS WITH DISABILITIES ACT OF 1990 (ADA)

This law makes it illegal to discriminate against a qualified person with a disability in the private sector and in state and local governments. The law also makes it illegal to retaliate against a person because the person complained about discrimination, filed a charge of discrimination, or participated in an employment discrimination investigation or lawsuit. The law also requires that employers reasonably accommodate the known physical or mental limitations of an otherwise qualified individual with a disability who is an applicant or employee, unless doing so would impose an undue hardship on the operation of the employer's business.

SECTIONS 102 AND 103 OF THE CIVIL RIGHTS ACT OF 1991

Among other things, this law amends Title VII and the ADA to permit jury trials and compensatory and punitive damage awards in intentional discrimination cases.

SECTIONS 501 AND 505 OF THE REHABILITATION ACT OF 1973

This law makes it illegal to discriminate against a qualified person with a disability in the federal government. The law also makes it illegal to retaliate against a person because the person complained about discrimination, filed a charge of discrimination, or participated in an employment discrimination investigation or lawsuit. The law also requires that employers reasonably accommodate the known physical or mental limitations of an otherwise qualified individual with a disability who is an applicant or employee, unless doing so would impose an undue hardship on the operation of the employer's business.

THE GENETIC INFORMATION NONDISCRIMINATION ACT OF 2008 (GINA)

This law makes it illegal to discriminate against employees or applicants because of genetic information. Genetic information includes information about an individual's genetic tests and the genetic tests of an individual's family members, as well as information about any disease, disorder or condition of an individual's family members (i.e. an individual's family medical history). The law also makes it illegal to retaliate against a person because the person complained about discrimination, filed a charge of discrimination, or participated in an employment discrimination investigation or lawsuit.

Source: www.eeoc.gov/statutes/laws-enforced-eeoc

EEOC Notification Response Checklist

RESOURCES

U.S. Equal Employment Opportunity Commission
  www.eeoc.gov/employers
  www.eeoc.gov/employers/what-you-can-expect-after-charge-filed
  www.eeoc.gov/employers/small-business/what-should-i-do-if-i-receive-eeoc-charge-discrimination

I-9 Error Corrections Checklist

PURPOSE

During I-9 self-audits, errors and mistakes on the forms may be discovered. There are specific ways in which to correct any errors. This *Ultimate HR Checklist* describes each Form I-9 section in detail and how to correct any errors. It is important to correct errors in the approved manner expected by Department of Homeland Security Immigration Customs and Enforcement (ICE). Failure to do so can lead to additional penalties and fines.

DEFINITIONS

I-9s: Officially the Employment Eligibility Verification, is a United States Citizenship and Immigration Services form. Mandated by the Immigration Reform and Control Act of 1986, it is used to verify the identity and legal authorization to work of all paid employees in the United States.

I-9 Error Corrections Checklist

CORRECTING SECTION 1—EMPLOYEE ONLY

- [ ] Notify employee in private of the specific deficiency
- [ ] Provide the I-9 Form to the employee with an explanation of the error/deficiency
- [ ] Errors in Section 1 should be corrected only by the employee
  - Employees should draw a line through the incorrect information
  - Enter the correct information
  - Initial and date the correction
  - If an employee needs assistance
  - Translator/preparer should draw a line through incorrect info
  - Translator/preparer enters or writes correct info
  - Employee initials and dates correct information
  - Translator/preparer initials and dates next to employees' initials
  - DO NOT use correction fluid
  - If you do accidentally use correction fluid, attach a signed and dated note to the corrected Forms I-9 explaining what happened
- [ ] If an employee is no longer working for you, attach a signed and dated statement
  - Identify the error or omission
  - Explain why corrections could not be made (no longer employed)
  - Make a note of the situation on your Audit Sheet

CORRECTING SECTION 2 AND 3—EMPLOYER ONLY

- [ ] Employers may only correct errors made in Section 2 or Section 3
- [ ] Draw a line through the incorrect information
- [ ] Enter the correct information
- [ ] Initial and date the correction
- [ ] DO NOT use correction fluid
- [ ] If you accidentally use correction fluid, attach a signed and dated note to the corrected Forms I-9 explaining what happened.

I-9 Error Corrections Checklist

CORRECTING MULTIPLE OR SUBSTANTIAL ERRORS

- [ ] You may redo the section on a new I-9 Form
- [ ] A current I-9 Form should be used
- [ ] Attach new I-9 Form to the old Form. DO NOT destroy the old form
- [ ] A note should be included in the file regarding the reason you made changes to an existing Form I-9 or completed a new Form I-9
- [ ] DO NOT use correction fluid
- [ ] If you accidentally use correction fluid, attach a signed and dated note to the corrected Forms I-9 explaining what happened.
- [ ] DO NOT back-date the form except for the actual date employment began

IF AN E-VERIFY ERROR IS FOUND

- [ ] If E-Verify WAS NOT in use when the employee was hired, DO NOT create a new case
- [ ] If E-Verify WAS in use when the employee was hired:
  - Create a case for them immediately
  - Choose the appropriate reason for creating a case outside the 3-day window—*Audit Revealed that New Hire Was Not Run*
  - Make a note on your Audit Sheet and attach a note to the I-9

I-9 Error Corrections Checklist

LEGAL CONCERNS

IMMIGRATION REFORM AND CONTROL ACT OF 1986 (IRCA)

IRCA prohibits employers from hiring and employing an individual for employment in the U.S. knowing that the individual is not authorized concerning such employment. Employers are also prohibited from employing an individual knowing that they are unauthorized for employment. This law also prohibits employers from hiring any individual, including a U.S. citizen, for employment in the U.S. without verifying their identity and employment authorization on Form I-9.

Federal law requires that every employer who recruits, refers for a fee, or hires an individual for employment in the U.S. must complete Form I-9, Employment Eligibility Verification. Form I-9 will help you verify your employee's identity and employment authorization.

RESOURCES

U.S. Citizenship and Immigration Services
www.uscis.gov/i-9-central
www.uscis.gov/i-9-central/form-i-9-resources/handbook-for-employers-m-274

I-9 Internal Audit Checklist

PURPOSE

Doing an I-9 self-audit every year is a best practice to be prepared should the Department of Homeland Security Immigration Customs and Enforcement (ICE) decide to visit your organization and ask to see the Forms. This *Ultimate HR Checklist* provides a list of steps to follow to conduct your self-audit. There is also a specific way to correct any errors. Be sure to reference the I-9 Completion *Ultimate HR Checklist* and I-9 Pitfalls *Ultimate HR Checklist* for additional information.

DEFINITIONS

I-9s: Officially the Employment Eligibility Verification, is a United States Citizenship and Immigration Services form. Mandated by the Immigration Reform and Control Act of 1986, it is used to verify the identity and legal authorization to work of all paid employees in the United States.

I-9 Internal Audit Checklist

ACTIVE EMPLOYEES

- [ ] Gather all I-9 for Active employees hired after November 6, 1986
- [ ] Create a list of all missing I-9's
- [ ] Review active employee I-9's to ensure proper completion
- [ ] Separate I-9s that have errors, missing sections, or missing documents
- [ ] Create an Audit Log with three columns—employee name, errors found, actions taken.
- [ ] Do not write on the I-9 Form. Use "sticky notes" to notate each error
- [ ] Contact all active employees who have missing I-9s or active employees that have incomplete or incorrect I-9's
- [ ] Explain the situation to the engaged employees and that the I-9 form needs to be filled out per federal law. Be honest and forthright.
- [ ] Show the employee their I-9 with the needed corrections and have them make the corrections (see Making I-9 Corrections Checklist)
- [ ] For employees that are missing an I-9 form, obtain a copy of the most recent Form I-9 and present it to them to fill out
- [ ] Fill out the employer section and Verify their ID's
- [ ] Do not back-date the form except for their start-date on page 2
- [ ] Attach a dated and signed note to the I-9 signifying that this is a replacement due to the loss of the original
- [ ] Record the situation in the Audit Log
- [ ] Place all finished active employee I-9s together in a file or binder in alphabetical order.
- [ ] Audit once a month to pull out and relocate terminated employee I-9's

IF YOU USE E-VERIFY

- [ ] You still must run cases for *all* your employees
- [ ] If your audit shows that an employee case was never completed in E-verify, you can submit it past the three-day deadline
- [ ] Select this as the reason for submitting late verification
- [ ] Do not re-run current employees through E-Verify a second time
- [ ] Never go back and run E-Verify cases for employees who were hired when your company was not enrolled in the E-Verify service.

TERMINATED EMPLOYEES

- [ ] Print a list of terminated employees from the past three years
- [ ] Review all terminated employee I-9s and retain them using the following retention formula -*Three years after the hire date, or one year after the date employment ends, whichever is later.*
- [ ] I-9's NOT retained should be separated and destroyed by shredding
- [ ] Remaining terminated employee I-9s should be included and placed in a separate folder and evaluated once a month using the retention formula

FINAL I-9 AUDIT STEPS

- [ ] Document all communications/actions and place with the final audit paperwork to show good faith effort in case of an official audit
- [ ] Conduct a meeting with all stakeholders to discuss improvements
- [ ] All physical I-9s should be stored safely and securely (locked)
- [ ] Consider electronic storage alternatives

I-9 Internal Audit Checklist

LEGAL CONCERNS

IMMIGRATION REFORM AND CONTROL ACT OF 1986 (IRCA)

IRCA prohibits employers from hiring and employing an individual for employment in the U.S. knowing that the individual is not authorized with respect to such employment. Employers also are prohibited from continuing to employ an individual knowing that they are unauthorized for employment. This law also prohibits employers from hiring any individual, including a U.S. citizen, for employment in the U.S. without verifying their identity and employment authorization on Form I-9.

Federal law requires that every employer who recruits, refers for a fee, or hires an individual for employment in the U.S. must complete Form I-9, Employment Eligibility Verification. Form I-9 will help you verify your employee's identity and employment authorization.

RESOURCES

U.S. Citizenship and Immigration Services
www.uscis.gov/i-9-central
www.uscis.gov/i-9-central/form-i-9-resources/handbook-for-employers-m-274

USERRA Employer Obligations Checklist

PURPOSE

The Uniformed Services Employment and Reemployment Rights Act (USERRA) guarantees an employee returning from military service or training the right to be reemployed at their former job (or as nearly comparable a job as possible) with the same benefits.

USERRA applies to virtually all employers, regardless of size, including the Federal Government. While the information presented herein applies primarily to private employers, the statute has parallel provisions that apply to Federal, State, and Local Government employers.

DEFINITIONS

Military services: A person who is a member of, applies to be a member of, performs, has performed, applies to perform, or has an obligation to perform service in a uniformed.

USERRA Employer Obligations Checklist

- [ ] Did the service member give advance notice of military service to the employer? (This notice can be written or verbal.)
- [ ] Did the employer allow the service member a leave of absence? The employer cannot require that vacation or other personal leave be used.
- [ ] Upon the timely application for reinstatement, did the employer promptly reinstate the service member to his/her escalator position?
- [ ] Did the employer grant or accrue seniority as if the returning service member had been continuously employed? This applies to the rights and benefits determined by seniority, including the status rate of pay, pension vesting, and credit for the period for pension benefit computations.
- [ ] Did the employer delay or attempt to defeat a reemployment rights obligation by demanding documentation that did not then exist or was not then readily available?
- [ ] Did the employer provide training or retraining and other accommodations to persons with service-connected disabilities? If a disability could not be accommodated after reasonable efforts by the employer, did the employer reemploy the person in some other position they were qualified to perform, which is the "nearest approximation" of the position to which the person was otherwise entitled, in terms of status and pay, and with full seniority?
- [ ] Did the employer make reasonable efforts to train or otherwise qualify a returning service member for a position within the organization/company? If the person could not be qualified in a similar position, did the employer place the person in any other position of lesser status and paid which they were qualified to perform with full seniority?
- [ ] Did the employer grant the reemployed person pension plan benefits during military service?
- [ ] Did the employer provide health coverage upon request of a service member whose leave was more than 30 days? Did the employer continue coverage at the regular employee cost for service members whose leave was less than 31 days?
- [ ] Did the employer discriminate in employment against or take adverse employment action against any person who assisted in the enforcement of protection afforded any returning service member under this Statute?
- [ ] Did the employer in any way discriminate in employment, reemployment, retention in employment, promotion, or any benefit of employment based on past or present membership, the performance of service, application for service, or obligation for military service?

USERRA Employer Obligations Checklist

LEGAL CONCERNS

UNIFORMED SERVICES EMPLOYMENT AND REEMPLOYMENT RIGHTS ACT OF 1994 (USERRA)

USERRA is a federal statute that protects service members' and veterans' civilian employment rights. Among other things, under certain conditions, USERRA requires employers to put individuals back to work in their civilian jobs after military service. USERRA also protects service members from discrimination in the workplace based on their military service or affiliation.

Be aware that in a lot of states, there is additional regulation on how members of the military are treated at work.

RESOURCES

Servicemembers and Veterans Initiative
> www.justice.gov/crt-military/userra-statute

Your Rights Under USERRA
> www.dol.gov/sites/dolgov/files/VETS/legacy/files/USERRA_Private.pdf

USERRA Overview
> osc.gov/Services/Pages/USERRA.aspx

W-2 Prep Checklist

PURPOSE

As employers, we are required to annually to issue W-2 forms to all of our employees. This *Ultimate HR Checklist* will guide you to ensure that you are not missing any of the steps.

W-2 Prep Checklist

DATES TO REMEMBER

- [ ] W-2 forms are due to employees by January 31st
- [ ] W-2 forms are due to the Social Security Administration by January 31st

GATHER INFORMATION ABOUT THE EMPLOYER

- [ ] Employer ID Number (EIN)
- [ ] Employer Name
- [ ] Employer Address
- [ ] Control Number

GATHER INFORMATION ABOUT THE EMPLOYEES

- [ ] Gross Pay: Total Wages, tips, and other compensation
- [ ] Withholdings
- [ ] Social Security Wages
- [ ] Social Security Tax Withheld
- [ ] Medicare wages and tips
- [ ] Medicare Tax withheld
- [ ] Social Security Tips and allocated tips
- [ ] Other payments such as EIC payments
- [ ] Dependent care benefits
- [ ] Retirement Plan participation
- [ ] Other compensation such as uncollected social security, railroad retirement, Medicare tax, tips, or group life insurance
  - Elective deferrals to 401(k), 403(b), and other qualified retirement plans
  - Non-taxable sick pay
  - Golden parachute payments
  - Excludable reimbursed moving expenses
  - Contributions to medical saving accounts or health saving accounts
  - Non-statutory employee stock options
  - Designated Roth contributions under 401(k) or 403(b)

W-2 Prep Checklist

- [ ] Other deductions or compensation
- [ ] State and Local Information
  - State Wages
  - State income tax withheld
  - Local Wages
  - Local Income Tax withheld
  - Locality Name
- [ ] Register to use Business Services Online
- [ ] File W-2s online
- [ ] Verify Employees Social Security Numbers

MAIL W-2S

- [ ] Employee
- [ ] Federal
- [ ] State
- [ ] Local

W-2 Prep Checklist

LEGAL CONCERNS

Federal, State and Local governments require us to properly file our tax forms with the government entity. This checklist is designed to help you properly fill out the W-2 for your employees and the government.

RESOURCES

Internal Revenue Service
www.irs.gov/forms-pubs/about-form-w-2
www.irs.gov/instructions/iw2w3
www.irs.gov/pub/irs-pdf/iw2w3.pdf

Appendix—
Legal Pitfalls

Americans with Disabilities (ADA) Legal Pitfalls Checklist

PURPOSE

Companies can get in trouble if they fail to follow laws and guidelines. This Checklist is a list of common Pitfalls that get companies in trouble regarding the Americans with Disabilities Act (ADA) compliance.

Americans With Disabilities (ADA) Legal Pitfalls Checklist

YOUR COMPANY CAN GET INTO TROUBLE REGARDING THE ADA IF YOU...

- [ ] Do not have detailed Job Descriptions
- [ ] Ignore a request for Accommodation
- [ ] Deny a request without consideration
- [ ] Fail to engage in the Interactive Process
- [ ] Make fun or joke about someone's disability
- [ ] Do not make an accommodation because you are concerned about what others might think—employees or customers
- [ ] Are not consistent with your own practices and procedures
- [ ] Do not make a good faith effort
- [ ] Have inconsistent, or no documentation showing your efforts to follow-through and engage in the interactive process
- [ ] Fail to educate your supervisors and managers on their responsibilities regarding the ADA

FMLA Legal Pitfalls Checklist

PURPOSE

Companies can get in trouble if they fail to follow laws and guidelines. This Checklist is a list of common Pitfalls that get companies in trouble when it comes to FMLA. Finish the following sentence with each checklist item below:

FMLA Legal Pitfalls Checklist

YOUR COMPANY CAN GET INTO FMLA TROUBLE IF YOU...

- [ ] Fail to provide the General Notice of FMLA Rights (poster)
- [ ] Ignore a verbal notice of the need to take FMLA
- [ ] Do not educate your supervisors and managers about FMLA
- [ ] Allow employees to take extended time off for a covered event without informing them of FMLA and their right to use it
- [ ] Fail to recognize Loco Parentis
- [ ] Do not inform an employee of their rights (3 Days Out sick)
- [ ] Do not follow Doctor instructions
- [ ] Decide not to use the FMLA Forms from DOL
- [ ] Demand details of the medical diagnosis from the employee
- [ ] Are not handling Benefits properly while employees are on leave
- [ ] Take Adverse Action or retaliation in any form
- [ ] Allow an employee to work without a release from their doctor
- [ ] Pressure and employee to come back to work early
- [ ] Give the employee work to do (even if they volunteer)
- [ ] Try to convince an employee to not use FMLA or return early because you are short-staffed

I-9 Legal Pitfalls Checklist

PURPOSE

Companies can get in trouble if they fail to follow laws and guidelines. This Checklist is a list of common pitfalls that can get companies in trouble regarding Form I-9 compliance.

I-9 Legal Pitfalls Checklist

YOUR COMPANY CAN GET INTO TROUBLE REGARDING THE FORM I-9 IF YOU...

- ☐ Do not have an I-9 for EVERY employee hired after November 6, 1986
- ☐ Miss the 3-day window of having an employee verify their employment
- ☐ Do not complete all fields on the form (missing information)
- ☐ Use White-Out or any corrective cover-up for corrections
- ☐ Are inconsistent with the way you enter information on the Form
- ☐ Forget to fill in the Employee's start date on page 2
- ☐ Take expired ID's
- ☐ Making copies of certain ID's only
- ☐ Make ID copies for only certain employees
- ☐ Do not confirm your Temp Agencies are using I-9 forms
- ☐ Allow Temp Agencies to place illegal workers on your property
- ☐ Forget to monitor employees with expiring work permits
- ☐ Selectively use E-Verify only for certain
- ☐ Put current employees through E-Verify
- ☐ Fail to follow through on E-Verify Non-Confirmations
- ☐ Fail to do an I-9 self-audit every year
- ☐ Store your I-9s improperly
- ☐ Shred terminated employee I-9s before the federal law allows
- ☐ Cannot produce your I-9s properly for an audit by ICE

Gratitude

Writing a book is not a solitary occupation. Although there were many times Chuck and I struggled on our own, there were so many people who supported us in this journey.

Although we have never met Atul Gawande, it was his book *The Checklist Manifesto* that was the nucleus for this book. After reading it both Chuck and I wondered how we could bring the concept of checklists into the HR world. As we talked to numerous HR professionals, we realized we each had a set of individual checklists but there was not a comprehensive database that would help both the new and senior HR professional as well as the small business owner.

Chuck and I would like to thank our early readers who taught us so much during this process. They made the book better. Jennifer Ancevski, Becky Becker, Keith L. Hammond, PJ Ketcham Robinson, and Amy Wodaski.

We would like to thank our proofreader Rosemary Giovannalli who painstaking read and re-read through this book several times. Her HR knowledge and love of punctuation was invaluable.

We are also in debt to Samantha Westley who painstakingly edited the document, catching our mistakes, and pushing us to make it better for our readers. Any remaining mistakes are Chuck's and mine.

We asked Cronin Creative to make our checklists a book and they outdid themselves, to make it readable and easy to use.

Finally we would like to thank our family members who supported us during the last two years as we worked on this little project which took on a life of its own. Sorry for the late night and early morning phone calls.

— John Thalheimer, Co-Author of *The Ultimate Guide to HR: Checklists Edition*

The Team at HR Stories

The Team behind the Ultimate Guide to HR Stories, Chuck Simikian SHRM-SCP, SPHR and John Thalheimer, MS Org Leadership, are also the experts behind the Team at HR Stories.

The Team at HR Stories helps businesses, non-profits and government agencies better manage the employee experience by providing consultation, workshops and resources.

STRATEGIC CONSULTING

John Thalheimer, our strategic planning expert, has worked with non-profits, small businesses, and corporate human resources teams to create strategic plans to move the organization toward success. Using a straightforward approach, John works with the leaders of the team to define the strategic goals the organization needs to achieve to be successful, develop clear strategic initiatives and actions that the team will take forward, and discuss the importance of organizational values. And what makes John's approach unique, for the next twelve months, John continues to hold the team accountable and to help remove any barriers that may arise.

IN-HOUSE TRAINING

John and Chuck are both certified business trainers and facilitators who have help tens of thousands of HR Professionals, Small Business Owners, Organizational Leaders, and employees be better at their job through their workshops, seminars and classes. They provide workshops of Employment Law, Employee Management Best Practices, How to Excel in any workplace, Leading Teams, Communication, Supervising for the First Time, and many, many more.

ON-DEMAND WORKSHOPS FOR HR PROFESSIONALS.

We know HR Professionals are better when they have the best information to do their job well. We have created a library of some of the most important topics from How to Master Difficult Conversations, How to Retain Your Best Employees, Record Retention, to Managing A Sexual Harassment Investigation.

THE HR STORIES PODCAST

At the Team at HR Stories, we love the power of a good story to help illustrate a point, each week Chuck and John discuss the hot topics in HR and dive deep into a story that matters to anyone managing employees. They have discussed religious discrimination, sexual harassment, employee rights, unions, constructive discharge, and many more topics. They also take the time to answer listener questions.

OTHER RESOURCES

Small Business Guide to HR: Managing employees is a critical aspect of leading an organization. *A Small Business Guide to Managing Human Resources* is a primer to help Small Business Owners, Entrepreneurs, Non-Profit Leaders, Store Managers, Plant Managers, Office Managers, and anyone responsible for handling the HR aspects of running an organization.

This guide includes building the foundational documents, hiring the best employees, creating the best work environment, keeping your team safe, properly rewarding your employees, and building proper systems for your organization.

Stay Interviews: The stay interview is a proactive approach to help your organization retain employees by understanding why individuals are staying and what, if anything, might entice them to leave. The information gathered during the stay interview process can improve job postings, recognition programs, and organizational retention incentives.

This booklet will guide you through the Stay Interview Process and show you how you can keep more employees from leaving your employment.

The Team at HR Stories is recognized by SHRM to offer Professional Development Credits (PDC) for SHRM-CP® or SHRM-SCP® recertification activities.

www.TeamAtHRStories.com | email@teamathrstories.com

Listen Now with **HRStoriesPodcast.com**

Where There Is A Lesson In Every Story

Each week on the HR Stories Podcast, John Thalheimer and Chuck Simikian, the authors of the *Ultimate Book of HR, Checklists Edition*, discuss the stories impacting small business owners, non-profit leaders, and Human Resources practitioners and the actions businesses need to take to avoid the same fate.

In short, they bring the *Ultimate Book of HR, Checklist Edition* to life.

State Resources

State Resources

The Ultimate Book of HR Checklists is based on federal employment law—however various states have employment law variations. Here is a list of state resources that you might find helpful.....

STATE	TITLE AND ADDRESS	PHONE NUMBER	WEBSITES / EMAIL
Alabama	Commissioner Alabama Department of Labor 649 Monroe St Montgomery, AL 36131	334-242-8990 Fax: 334-242-3960	www.labor.alabama.gov
Alaska	Commissioner Department of Labor and Workforce Development PO Box 11149 Juneau, AK 99811-1149	907-465-2700 Fax: 907-465-2784	www.labor.state.ak.us commissioner.labor@alaska.gov
Arizona	Director Industrial Commission of Arizona 800 W Washington St Phoenix, AZ 85007	602-542-4515 Fax: 602-542-8097	www.azica.gov
Arkansas	Director, Division of Labor Arkansas Department of Labor & Licensing 10421 W Markham St Little Rock, AR 72205	501-682-4500 Fax: 501-682-4535	www.labor.arkansas.gov asklabor@arkansas.gov
California	Director 1515 Clay Street, Suite 1302 Oakland, CA 94612	1-844-522-6734 510-285-2118	www.dir.ca.gov/contactus.html
Colorado	Executive Director Department of Labor and Employment 633 17th St Suite 201 Denver, CO 80202-3660	303-318-8441 Fax: 303-318-8400	www.coloradolaborlaw.gov

STATE	TITLE AND ADDRESS	PHONE NUMBER	WEBSITES / EMAIL
Connecticut	Commissioner Department of Labor 200 Folly Brook Blvd Wethersfield, CT 06109-1114	860-263-6000 Fax: 860-263-6529	www.ct.gov/dol
Delaware	Director Division of Industrial Affairs 4425 N Market St 4th Floor Wilmington, DE 19802	302-761-8176 Fax: 302-761-6621	www.delawareworks.com
District of Columbia	Director Department of Employment Services 4058 Minnesota Ave NE Washington, DC 20019 Director DC Office of Human Rights 441 4th St NW Suite 570 North Washington, DC 20001	202-671-1900 Fax: 202-673-6993 202-727-4559 Fax: 202-727-9589	www.does.dc.gov ohr.dc.gov
Florida	Executive Director Florida Department of Economic Opportunity 107 E Madison St Tallahassee, FL 32399	850-245-7105 Fax: 850-921-3223	www.floridajobs.org
Georgia	Commissioner Department of Labor 148 Andrew Young International Blvd NE Sussex Place, Room 600 Atlanta, GA 30303	404-232-7300 Fax: 404-656-2683	www.dol.state.ga.us

STATE	TITLE AND ADDRESS	PHONE NUMBER	WEBSITES / EMAIL
Hawaii	Director Department of Labor & Industrial Relations Princess Ruth Ke'elikolani Building 830 Punchbowl St Room 321 Honolulu, HI 96813	808-586-8844 Fax: 808-586-9099	www.labor.hawaii.gov
Idaho	Director Idaho Department of Labor 317 W Main St Boise, ID 83735-0001	208-332-3579 Fax: 208-334-6430	www.labor.idaho.gov
Illinois	Acting Director Department of Labor 160 N LaSalle St 13th Floor, Suite C-1300 Chicago, IL 60601	312-793-2800 Fax: 312-793-5257	www2.illinois.gov/idol
Indiana	Commissioner Department of Labor 402 W. Washington St Room W195 Indianapolis, IN 46204	317-232-2655 Fax: 317-233-3790	www.in.gov/dol
Iowa	Labor Commissioner Iowa Workforce Development 1000 E Grand Ave Des Moines, IA 50319-0209	515-281-5915 Fax: 515-281-7995	www.iowaworkforce development.gov/
Kansas	Secretary Department of Labor 401 SW Topeka Blvd Topeka, KS 66603-3182	785-296-5000 Fax: 785-368-6294	www.dol.ks.gov

STATE	TITLE AND ADDRESS	PHONE NUMBER	WEBSITES / EMAIL
Kentucky	Secretary Kentucky Labor Cabinet Mayo-Underwood Building 500 Mero Street, 3rd Floor Frankfort, Kentucky 40601	502-564-3070 Fax: 502-564-5387	www.labor.ky.gov
Louisiana	Executive Director Louisiana Workforce Commission 1001 N 23rd St Baton Rouge, LA 70802	225-342-3111 Fax: 225-342-7960	www2.laworks.net
Maine	Commissioner Department of Labor 45 Commerce Dr Augusta, ME 04333	207-621-5095 Fax: 207-287-5292	www.maine.gov/labor
Maryland	Secretary Department of Labor, Licensing and Regulation 500 N Calvert St Suite 401 Baltimore, MD 21202	410-230-6020 Fax: 410-333-0853	www.dllr.state.md.us
Massachusetts	Secretary Executive Office of Labor & Workforce Development One Ashburton Pl Room 2112 Boston, MA 02108 Chief Fair Labor Division, Office of the Attorney General One Ashburton Pl Boston, MA 02108	617-626-7122 Fax: 617-727-1090 617-727-3465	www.mass.gov/eolwd

STATE	TITLE AND ADDRESS	PHONE NUMBER	WEBSITES / EMAIL
Michigan	Director Department of Labor and Economic Opportunity 105 W Allegan St Lansing, MI 48933	517-241-6712	www.michigan.gov/lara
Minnesota	Commissioner Department of Labor and Industry 443 Lafayette Rd N St. Paul, MN 55155	651-284-5075 Fax: 651-284-5725	www.dli.mn.gov
Mississippi	Executive Director Department of Employment Security 1235 Echelon Pkwy PO Box 1699 Jackson, MS 39215-1699	601-321-6000 Fax: 601-321-6004	www.mdes.ms.gov
Missouri	Director Labor and Industrial Relations Commission 421 E Dunklin St PO Box 504 Jefferson City, MO 65102-0504	573-751-4091 Fax: 573-751-4135	www.labor.mo.gov
Montana	Commissioner Department of Labor and Industry PO Box 1728 Helena, MT 59624-1728	406-444-2840 Fax: 406-444-1419	www.dli.mt.gov
Nebraska	Commissioner Department of Labor 550 S 16th St PO Box 94600 Lincoln, NE 68508-4600	402-471-9000 Fax: 402-471-2318	www.dol.nebraska.gov

STATE	TITLE AND ADDRESS	PHONE NUMBER	WEBSITES / EMAIL
Nevada	Commissioner Department of Business and Industry 555 E Washington Ave Suite 4100 Las Vegas, NV 89101-1050	775-486-2650 Fax: 775-486-2660	labor.nv.gov
New Hampshire	Commissioner Department of Labor 95 Pleasant St Concord, NH 03301	603-271-3176 Fax: 603-271-6852	www.nh.gov/labor/
New Jersey	Commissioner Department of Labor and Workforce Development 1 John Fitch Plaza 13th Floor, Suite D PO Box 110 Trenton, NJ 08625-0110	609-659-9045 Fax: 609-633-9271	www.nj.gov/labor/
New Mexico	Acting Secretary Department of Work Force Solutions 401 Broadway Blvd NE PO Box 1928 Albuquerque, NM 87102-1928	Fax: 505-841-8491	www.dws.state.nm.us
New York	Commissioner Department of Labor State Office Bldg # 12 W.A. Harriman Campus Albany, NY 12240	518-457-9000 Fax: 518-457-6908	www.labor.ny.gov
North Carolina	Commissioner Department of Labor 4 W Edenton St Raleigh, NC 27601	800-625-2267 Fax: 888-733-9389	www.labor.nc.gov

STATE	TITLE AND ADDRESS	PHONE NUMBER	WEBSITES / EMAIL
North Dakota	Commissioner North Dakota Department of Labor 600 E Boulevard Ave Dept 406 Bismarck, ND 58505-0340	701-328-2660 Fax: 701-328-2031	www.nd.gov/labor
Ohio	Director Department of Commerce 77 S High St 23rd Floor Columbus, OH 43215	614-644-2239 Fax: 614-466-5650	com.ohio.gov
Oklahoma	Commissioner Department of Labor 3017 N Stiles Ave Suite 100 Oklahoma City, OK 73105-5212	405-521-6100 Fax: 405-521-6018	www.labor.ok.gov
Oregon	Commissioner-Elect Bureau of Labor and Industries 800 NE Oregon St #1045 Portland, OR 97232	971-673-0761 Fax: 971-673-0762	www.oregon.gov/boli
Pennsylvania	Secretary Department of Labor and Industry 651 Boas St 1700 Labor and Industry Bldg Harrisburg, PA 17121	717-787-5279 Fax: 717-787-8826	www.dli.state.pa.us
Rhode Island	Director Department of Labor and Training 1511 Pontiac Ave Cranston, RI 02920	401-462-8550 Fax: 401-462-8872	www.dlt.ri.gov

STATE	TITLE AND ADDRESS	PHONE NUMBER	WEBSITES / EMAIL
South Carolina	Director Department of Labor, Licensing & Regulations 110 Centerview Dr Columbia, SC 29210-1329	803-896-4300 Fax: 803-896-4393	www.llr.state.sc.us
South Dakota	Secretary Department of Labor and Regulation 700 Governors Dr Pierre, SD 57501-2291	605-773-3101 Fax: 605-773-6184	www.dlr.sd.gov
Tennessee	Commissioner Department of Labor & Workforce Development 220 French Landing Dr Nashville, TN 37243	844-224-5818 Fax: 615-253-8903	www.tn.gov/workforce
Texas	Commissioner Representing Labor Texas Workforce Commission 101 E 15th St Room 651 Austin, TX 78778-0001	512-475-2670 Fax: 512-475-2152	www.twc.state.tx.us
Utah	Commissioner Utah Labor Commission 160 E 300 S Suite 300 PO Box 146600 Salt Lake City, UT 84111-6600	801-530-6800 Fax: 801-530-6390	www.laborcommission.utah.gov
Vermont	Commissioner Department of Labor 5 Green Mountain Dr PO Box 488 Montpelier, VT 05601-0488	802-828-4000 Fax: 802-828-4022	www.labor.vermont.gov

STATE	TITLE AND ADDRESS	PHONE NUMBER	WEBSITES / EMAIL
Virginia	Commissioner Department of Labor and Industry 600 E Main St Suite 207 Richmond, VA 23219-4101	804-371-2327 Fax: 804-786-2376	www.doli.Virginia.gov
Washington	Director Department of Labor and Industries 7273 Linderson Way SW Tumwater, WA 98501-5414 PO Box 44000 Olympia, WA 98504-4000	360-902-5800 Fax: 360-902-5708	www.lni.wa.gov
West Virginia	Commissioner Division of Labor 1900 Kanawha Blvd State Capitol Complex Building #3 Room 200 Charleston, WV 25305	304-558-7890 Fax: 304-558-2273	labor.wv.gov
Wisconsin	Transition Director Department of Workforce Development 201 E Washington Ave #A400 Madison, WI 53703 PO Box 7946 Madison, WI 53707-7946	608-266-3131 Fax: 608-266-1784	dwd.wisconsin.gov
Wyoming	Director Department of Workforce Services 1510 E Pershing Blvd Cheyenne, WY 82002	307-777-8728 Fax: 307-777-5857	www.wyomingworkforce.org

STATE	TITLE AND ADDRESS	PHONE NUMBER	WEBSITES / EMAIL
Guam	Director Department of Labor PO Box 9970 Tamuning, GU 96931-9970	671-475-7043	dol.guam.gov/
Northern Mariana Islands	Secretary of Labor Capitol Hill Saipan, MP 96950	670-323-9932 Fax: 670-664-3197	www.marianaslabor.net
Puerto Rico	Secretary Department of Labor and Human Resources Edificio Prudencio Rivera Martinez 505 Muniz Rivera Ave GPO Box 3088 Hato Rey, PR 00918	787-754-2120	www.trabajo.pr.gov
Virgin Islands	Commissioner Department of Labor 2203 Church St St. Croix, VI 00802-4612	St. Croix: 340-692-9689 St. Thomas: 340-776-3700	www.vidol.gov

Information provided by the DOL at www.dol.gov/agencies/whd/state/contacts

www.ingramcontent.com/pod-product-compliance
Lightning Source LLC
Chambersburg PA
CBHW040003040426
42337CB00033B/5208